Official Know-It-All Guide™

Mortgage Maze

Your Absolute, Quintessential,
All You Wanted to Know,
Complete Guide

Cedric H. Campbell

Frederick Fell Publishers, Inc.

Fell's Official Know-It-All Guide

Frederick Fell Publishers, Inc.

2131 Hollywood Boulevard, Suite 305

Hollywood, Florida 33020

954-925-5242

e-mail: fellpub@aol.com

Visit our Web site at www.fellpub.com

This publication is designed to provide accurate and authoritative information in regard to the subject matter covered. It is sold with the understanding that the publisher is not engaged in rendering legal, accounting, or other professional service. If legal advice or other assistance is required, the services of a competent professional person should be sought. From A Declaration of Principles jointly adopted by a Committee of the American Bar Association and a Committee of Publishers.

Library of Congress Cataloging-in-Publication Data

Campbell,Cedric H., 1958-
 The mortage maze : survival guide to financing and re financing
your home / by Cedric H. Campbell.
  p. cm.-- (Fell's official know-it-all guide)
  Includes bibliographical references.
  ISBN 0-88391-059-4
  1. Mortgage loans. 2. Mortgages. 3. Mortgage
loans--Refinancing.   I. Title. II. Series.
  HG2040. 15 .C36 2001
  332.7'22--dc21

                              2001005066

Cover graphics and interior design by: Carey Jacobs

Author's Comments:

I originally introduced readers to the Mortgage Maze in the middle years of the 1980's. It was my way of informing them of the twists and turns, perils and potholes of the mortgage process. Simply put, it was intended to level the playing field between those who establish the rules (lenders) and those who are subject to them (borrowers). It was distributed to friends, family members, and an intimate circle of business associates.

Twenty years later, I found myself in a position of refinancing my home. I found it interesting that although the calendar and technology were in balance, the playing field was clearly tilted. Ironically my neighbors, family members and friends participating in the "refi" boom were all experiencing this phenomenon. They looked to my experience and me to find solace. One of my neighbors credited me and suggested I write a book on the subject. I thought about it for a moment, dusted off an earlier copy and remembered I already did.

Acknowledgement
&
Dedication

To those who inspired me in the late

1980's to write the initial Mortgage Maze,

I thank you.

To Bonnie who supported and

encouraged me in the late evening hours

to offer a revision,

I embrace you.

iv

Contents

Chapters

1 Your First Steps into the Maze 1

Gathering Information: Assessing Your Needs * Looking
at Loans * Basic Information * Kinds of Lenders * Kinds of
Loans * Fixed Rate Mortgages * Adjustable Rate Mortgages
* Combinations and Variations * Convertable Loans * Adver-
tised Specials * Loan Limits * Getting Technical on Rates
* Continuing Your Research

2 A Companion for the Trip 19

Choosing a Loan Agent: Framing Your Questions * Looking
at Lenders * Banks and Savings Banks * Thrift and Loan
Associations * Credit Unions * Mortgage Bankers and Mortgage
Brokers * Finding the Lending Agent for You * Learning from
Others Who've Been through the Maze * Looking at Companies
and Institutions * Getting a Picture of Loan Officers and Agents
*Making Your Decision

Chapters

Chapters

5 Light at the End of the Tunnel 91

Approving the Loan: The Four C's * Credit and Capacity
*Collateral * Condition * Questions About the Four C's * After
the Four C's * The Final Decision

6 Out of the Maze 105

Closing the Loan: Reviewing Legal Documents * Grant
Deed * Deed of Trust * Note or Security Instrument * Adjustable Rate Mortgage * Settlement Statement/HUD 1 * Notice
to Recind * Recording the Loan * Signing the Papers * Living
with Your Loan

Summary 132

Note: The author uses the term "mortgage" throughout this book. In California and many other states 'Trust Deeds" have replaced mortgages as the security instrument. Notwithstanding, the word "mortgage" is more commonly used in the industry hence the decision.

Preface

During my senior year at San Diego State University, I made a conscious decision never to work in sales, finance, or real estate. So much for that thought: Here I am many years later in the very heart of the business I promised myself I'd stay away from. But, you know, I wouldn't change a single thing.

After obtaining my Bachelor's degree in marketing, I set course as an Account Executive for Citicorp selling mortgages. At that time, I could have made you happy if I could secure for you a mortgage at 21% and 3 points. I would have been your best friend if I could get a rate of 18% and 5 points.

I guess I did something right because I was placed in our home office in St. Louis, Missouri as a Regional Training Specialist. It was there that I had the opportunity to develop my expertise in mortgage lending. I was involved in product development, product training, and best of all, working with hundreds of experts willing to share their experiences with me. For all intents and purposes, I became the SME (subject matter expert) for the Western region. I received my Master's degree while in Arizona, and my role in the company became one of fire fighter and problem solver. Technically, I was given the title of Regional Sales Manager, but I received two things that gave me much more satisfaction: the chance to work with all the departments of the company and the opportunity to interview well over 100 real estate professional throughout the country, trying to discover just what they needed to be successful. That's when I discovered the true secret of the concept of customer service.

I later joined The Gibraltar Money Center as a District Manager/Underwriter. My task was very simple: increase sales in California's Orange County. It was there that I learned all about portfolio underwriting and being responsible for underwriting decisions. At GMCI, I was responsible for establishing the goals and direction for business development and for creating a high quality loan portfolio. I developed an assertive wholesale origination unit and directed it through a sales strategy, which catapulted our market share, position from 113th to 28th. I could generate business, and I was aware of prudent portfolio loan management and expense control. I escalated GMCI's loan portfolio from $7.0 million to $44.0 million with less than a 2% delinquency in a short 24 months. And that was done with second mortgages only and generally with more difficult to place loans. After a company downsizing, I took on a short stewardship with Home Savings of America. As Vice President Regional Sales Administrator, I took my eight lending offices to more than $1.2 billion in residential loan sales.

Then I did what every entrepreneur does. I tested my entrepreneurial spirit. I owned and operated a small but healthy wholesale mortgage operation. We built our entire business plan on one thing: the simple belief that without serving our clients the very best we can and without meeting their expectations, we have no reason to be in existence. It was a lot of hard work when you consider economic and competitive pressures but it was also a heck of a lot of fun to make a customer smile. For many, the economic pressures felt in California was too much. And it was for me too. After the earthquakes, fires, floods, and riots of Southern California I closed shop and returned to my roots at Citibank. As the Director of Telesales at Citibank, I was introduced to the forward thinking of virtual banking and alternative distribution systems. Directing a small group of telemarketers we designed an infrastructure, which increased sales from $81 million to $181 million in 14 months. Despite success, I turned my focus to my personal life by moving back to Southern California marrying my wonderful wife Bonnie and taking on the challenges of the subprime market. This is the market segment that is comprised of individuals who have suffered financial hardships thus causing deterioration in their credit history.

After a quick start with a local Thrift & Loan, and then the head of retail efforts for one the largest mortgage lenders in the country I made a decision to step out of the lending arena and jump on the technology band wagon where I work as an independent consultant to mortgage bankers who seek technological direction. But despite my decision to leave a large stable corporate environment, explore my entrepreneurial spirit, return to the strength of a major lender, then head on my own again, the commitment to the plan has never changed. That plan, a commitment to make sure that we as real estate professionals do everything we can to support the well being of those who hired us: you—the client, the potential home buyer, the newlyweds facing the unknown, the empty nesters who have been forced to adapt to change.

My reason for writing The Mortgage Maze grew out of that commitment. We can't serve you if we keep our knowledge to ourselves, and you have only fragments and maybe some misconceptions. We, as an industry, have not done our best to meet our responsibility for sharing the information you need to make well-informed decisions. We must do better. The Mortgage Maze is, therefore, my way of sharing with you the experience of the thousands of experts who have succeeded, you and I will both profit- not simply in terms of dollars and cents but more rewardingly in terms of time and satisfaction. We will enjoy the process and the results of getting through the maze to the best possible home mortgage.

I do hope that the guidebook works well for you. I do hope that you will let me know how it helped you through the mortgage maze.

Cedric H. Campbell

INTRODUCTION

LOOKING INTO THE MAZE

When I was a child, I enjoyed working my way through the mazes that appeared in magazines. There were dead ends and confusing turns; it was easy to get lost or go wrong and lose time. Those mazes were as frustrating as they were exciting; they were as exciting as they were frustrating.

Getting a house financed or refinanced today can be as frustrating as home ownership is exciting. You have probably heard or read about (or experienced) all kinds of horror stories. They sound something like the following composites.

While shopping for rates, a borrower was told by different lenders why their loans were cheaper than the other guy's. When the customer asked one whether he could guarantee the rate, he said "yes," and the loan was started. Later, the rate was increased, and the customer learned that a rate could be guaranteed if it was "locked," but his rate wasn't locked.

One lending agent explained six possible loans and recommended one as best for the applicant. The applicant tried to get a comparison price on that loan from another lender, who said, "Oh my, why would you ever want that loan in your situation? It's wrong for you for three reasons." And the loan that agent recommended was called the wrong one by the next lender. And so on.

The loan application was most complicated because three single individuals, each with involved and unusual incomes, were buying a house together. The forms filled several folders, making a stack over a foot high. The entire file was lost, including original documents.

The lender or the lender's agent never called the applicant with instructions or updates but complained if the applicant didn't supply information or dared to ask about the progress of the loan.

The lender or the lender's agent called every third day for more and more documentation-often something that had already been submitted or was most difficult to provide. The applicant was asked for photocopies of cancelled checks (both sides) for all mortgage payments made in the last year because the spouse who wrote all the checks used a different name. That was the only thing holding up the loan, but the applicant's bank used checkbooks with carbon copies, charged a dollar a check to photocopy cancelled checks on file, and took three weeks to make copies. Three years after a loan was made, the customers were informed that the loan was due and payable. The wife and husband reviewed their note and deed and found to their dismay that they received a 30-year loan with a three-year balloon. They called the original lender to discuss the problem, only to learn that the company was out of business and they were at the mercy of the old loan.

A process that should have been completed in less than a month dragged on two, three, four months and more, during which time bad things began happening. First, these first-time homebuyers got caught in a squeeze because they had given notice at their apartment house, and the owner there rented the apartment and insisted that it be vacated. Then rates went up. Next, the lender wanted to update items on the application, which was like starting all over.

The loan went through, but there were strange new costs for getting the loan, and the size of the loan was increased by $7,000 to cover those costs, making payments higher for the life of the loan.

The loan went through, but it was a thirty-year fixed loan at 7.875% rather than the balloon loan at 6.75% as discussed. The lender's agent offered a vague explanation having to do with the nature of the property, leaving the applicant to decide whether to accept the higher rate or start the process all over with another agent or lender.

A customer's loan was approved, but the rate that was quoted was not available, and the loan agent did not tell the client. Eventually, the rate was made available. So much time had passed, however, that the lender reviewed the appraisal and found that the value of the property had decreased by $15,000. To get the loan, the client would have to supply a cashier's check for the $15,000.

After weeks of waiting, the applicant was turned down because some rule or regulation or practice was changed. A seasoned agent would have known andadvised the client, but an uninformed rookie agent promised the applicant the world.

And on they go, one horror story after another. That is the reason I have prepared this guidebook:

To get you through the Mortgage Maze.

When I was working my way through those printed mazes, I discovered that it is easier to start at the end and go back to the beginning. With a child's game, it is more fun and more challenging-and sporting-to start at the beginning and pick one's way through. With a mortgage, it is best to start at the beginning (gathering of information), in the middle (processing the loan), and at the end (closing of the loan) to be certain that you are on the right path all the way.

At this point, you may well ask, "Why must getting a mortgage require picking one's way through a maze? Shouldn't the process be more like planning a trip on established roads than dealing with deliberate dead ends? Or do lenders want it to be a maze?"

A full answer to that question would call for a book or two. The short answer is that all business has become more complicated. Until the 1950s, almost everyone who wanted a mortgage went to a bank, and the bank's officers looked at the application and made a decision. (Often the decision was based on family name or reputation; those were known as "good old boy" loans.) Then, in the next four decades, savings and loan institutions sprang up, thrift associations appeared, credit unions came on the scene, other kinds of institutions invested in mortgages, private lenders became players, and government agencies became involved.

Each group had its own objectives. Banks wanted to make money for owners or stockholders. S&L's wanted to do the same and also pay dividends to savers. Credit Unions wanted to serve members of specific groups (teachers, telephone company workers, and so on). Private lenders, insurance companies, pension fund managers and others looked at mortgages as they might look at the stock market. Government agencies were established to regulate certain practices, to make home ownership more readily available, or to insure loans to circulate credit.

As expanding markets and a vibrant economy in the 1960s and 1970s saw increased house sales, commercial interests sought new ways to make money. Adjustable rate mortgages offered one way to increase the number of homebuyers. "Creative financing" of the 1970s and 1980s got more people into houses (and some into trouble). Home equity loans became popular in the 1980s. Then, as the economy slowed and faltered, various bad practices by banks and S&L's came to light, practices that produced bad loans and federal intercession.

The S&L's that survived quit using Savings and Loan as part of their titles. They became Uptown Savings or Uptown Savings Bank when, because of specific loopholes, they acquired the right to offer banking services (such as money market accounts and retirement funds).

All those forces made getting a mortgage loan more complicated. Lenders, concerned about bad loans, began asking for more documentation, more evidence of ability and willingness to pay. Government agencies added regulations to protect buyers from unfair practices and from discrimination. Loan agents, trying to satisfy lenders and regulators, added complications. All those activities put new loads on escrow companies and title insurance companies, which had to protect themselves with added procedures. The result is a ton of paperwork and dozens of rules for each loan, and that in itself creates a maze. A mortgage maze.

A conscientious, efficient, well-informed loan officer can get you through the process, but first, you have to find that person, and second, instead of simply putting your mortgage, your money, and your future, into the hands of a loan officer and hoping for the best, you should know enough about the process to protect yourself and your interests. It is your money and ultimately your responsibility.

This guidebook has been prepared to get you through the mortgage maze. It does not show you all the sights or give you all the history. It would require several separate books to explain the business of lending, the setting of interest rates from Federal Reserve to the local bank, credit rating and reports, government regulations, and other structures and procedures you'll encounter along the way. The guidebook does make brief stops to tell you what you must know to get all the way through the maze.

> NOTE: Throughout the guidebook, the word "you" refers to the person or persons whose name or names will be on the mortgage and the deed: an individual, spouses, partners .... If wife and husband are applying, you always mean both spouses.

The first chapter is a picture of present day financing and refinancing of mortgages. It shows you how to begin thinking concretely about the kind of loan you need in your situation and what information you'll need to apply for that loan. The second chapter treats the task of choosing among the many lenders and loan agents who all say that they offer the best available loans. The third chapter takes you through the process of completing a loan application that gives you your best chance for loan approval. The fourth and fifth chapters tell you what happens in that dreadful waiting period before you get a response from the lender on your application. The sixth chapter explains the closing of an approved loan.

Some of the information will be familiar to some readers. You won't have to spend as much time with the familiar parts as with the unfamiliar, but do be certain that you don't skim over something new or different in a familiar section.

If most of the book seems familiar, then you have confirmation that your information is valid.

Whether you read the book alone or with someone, with a pen in hand at the kitchen table or in your favorite couch, I'm confident that your trip through the maze will be a rewarding experience.

Chapter One

Your First Steps into the Maze:

Gathering Information

You've decided to buy a house or refinance the one you're in-or you're thinking about it. You're outside the mortgage maze looking in. You may be eager or reluctant, confident or afraid, well-informed or poorly informed, but you will step in.

Before you do, you should assess your needs and get a clear and current picture of the business of getting a loan. The more and better information you gather before you start, the easier it will be to get through the maze.

<u>Assessing Your Needs</u>

Simply because interest rates are low or because thousands and millions of people are buying or refinancing houses, those aren't adequate reasons for your doing so. Your reasons should be right for you in your present situation: your plans and wishes, your income and obligations.

As a guide, respond to the questions that follow. Write your responses so that you can look at them, analyze them, rewrite them, and communicate them to a lending agent. The human brain is so fast, so agile, that it can handle contradictions and vague thoughts that you'll catch when they are on paper.

Each person whose name will be on the mortgage should write responses; then all responses should be compared and discussed.

➤ Where would you like to be one year from now? Five years from now? Ten years from now?

➤ What would you like to be doing one year from now? Five years from now? Ten years from now?

➤ How much longer would you like to live in your present residence?

➤ Would you prefer to remodel your present house or move to another house?

➤ Will your family continue to grow, or will you have an empty nest in a few years or in several years?

➤ What are the needs of your children, their children, or others about whom you must be concerned?

➤ What is the likelihood your job might require you to move?

➤ Will your income likely remain the same? Increase? Decrease?

➤ What are your present financial obligations? How much on a mortgage? How much on installment buying? How much on personal loans? How much on credit cards?

➤ How much additional financial responsibility can you handle on a mortgage obligation?

➤ Will a new mortgage deplete your savings?

➤ What do you most need in a new mortgage: lower total obligation, lower interest rate, lower monthly payments, or cash?

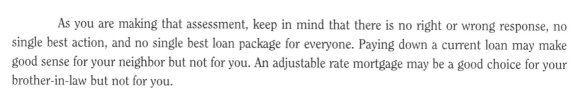

➤ If you are refinancing to get cash, do you have a specific plan for that cash?

➤ Are there still other considerations in your case?

As you are making that assessment, keep in mind that there is no right or wrong response, no single best action, and no single best loan package for everyone. Paying down a current loan may make good sense for your neighbor but not for you. An adjustable rate mortgage may be a good choice for your brother-in-law but not for you.

You will use your assessment to make decisions before you start the process and to get yourself ready for the process. Your loan agent will use your information to help you find the best loan offering for you.

Looking at Loans

As was noted in the Introduction, getting a home mortgage is not as simple today as it was when everything was limited to fixed rate financing and the mortgage loan was usually obtained from the bank which handled all of the customer's banking needs. Consider the emergence of the Internet and what was intended to be easy can be perceived to complex.

Not only are there more kinds of lenders and more kinds of loans but also more movement of mortgage money and new variations and combinations of loans. Lenders aren't necessarily sitting on available money; they have sources of money-often the same sources that all other lenders have-and they are very likely to make a loan and then sell that loan to another company. (More on that later.)

It seems that each week brings a new way that lenders can make money available or a new way of reading percentages or a new way that interest rates can be structured. Mortgage seekers are offered more and more options, each designed for specific needs and for a specific economy.

You cannot be expected to be aware of all those changes and of all the possibilities that are available, but if you understand general requirements and practices and the major kinds of loans, you and the lending agent will understand each other much more clearly and will move much more quickly toward getting the best loan package for you.

3

Basic Information

If you have never bought a house, townhouse, condominium-any piece of residential property-or it has been a very long time since you took on a mortgage, we'd better make a few basic points.

> A **mortgage** is a formal and legal commitment that a borrower will repay a loan advanced for the purchase of a piece of property. The mortgage document sets forth all the terms of repayment, including principal and interest.

> The **principal** is the amount of the debt, exclusive of accrued interest, remaining on a loan. At the outset, the principal is the total amount of the loan.

> The **loan balance** is the amount still owed on the principal after the last monthly payment.

> **Interest** is the charge the borrower pays for using the lender's money. Interest is paid on the full

principal and is expressed as a percentage rate (7%, for example).

➢ **Interest rates** are determined by the nation's economy, going up and down as the economy goes up and down. That may be all that you need to know, but if you want to understand a complex process that involves the Federal Reserve Board, stock markets, banks, you have to think of money as a commodity that is bought and sold. You might want to say, "Wait a minute. Money is the means of buying other things. How can money be bought and sold?" Well, look in the business section of your newspaper, among the stock market quotations, for a chart that shows "Money Rates." There, you'll see "bank prime rate," "discount rate," "federal funds rate," and several other rates that show what the biggest players are paying to use someone else's money. By the time that you get to use someone else's money, the interest rate will be two or three percentage points higher. If rates among the big players go up, the rates to homebuyers go up quickly. If rates among the big players go down, there will likely be a lag time before the rates for homebuyers go down.

➢ The **monthly payment** is an amount that pays both principal and interest. With a *fixed rate mortgage (FRM)*, the monthly payment remains the same for the life of the loan. (In the section below on fixed rate mortgages, there is an example of monthly payments and the relative amounts that go to principal and interest.) With an *adjustable rate mortgage (ARM)*, the monthly payment may increase or decrease as the economy changes.

➢ **Loan** *fees* are the cost of getting the loan and are discussed in Chapters Four and Five. The major fee is termed Loan Origination Fee or points. One *point* is 1 % of the principal. Loan fees can be very confusing and can raise the cost of the loan by hundreds or thousands of dollars.

Kinds of Lenders

You have more choices today than ever before. Choosing from among lenders and lending agents is covered in Chapter Two.

Kinds of Loans

The two major kinds of loans are still the fixed and the adjustable rate loans, each with its basic characteristics:

Fixed Rate Mortgages (FRM)	Adjustable Rate Mortgages (ARM)
Payments remain constant	Payments may change periodically
Principal reduction guaranteed	Principal reduction not guaranteed
Interest rate remains the same	Interest rate can change

Fixed Rate Mortgages

5

The old-fashioned Fixed Rate Mortgage (FRM), in effect, adds the interest to be paid over the life of the loan to the principal of the loan. The interest on a $100,000 loan at 7% to be paid off in 30 years (360 months) would be $139,508, making the total cost $239,508. The monthly payment would be approximately $665.30. Here is the way the payment process works.

For the first payment, multiply the balance owed ($100,000) by 7% to determine the first year's interest ($7,000) and divide that by 12 to find the first month's interest ($583.33). The remainder of the payment ($665.30 - $583.33 = $81.97) reduces the principal, so subtract that from the balance owed for a new balance

of $99,918.03. For the next month, take 7% of the new balance, divide that by 12 to see what the interest will be for that month, then subtract the interest from the monthly payment. Subtract the rest of the payment from the principal to get the new balance. Repeat that process for each month.

At the outset nearly all the payment goes to interest and very little to reducing the principal. The amount going to principal increases a few pennies each month, and it takes many years before most of the payment goes to principal. On that $100,000 loan at 7%, here are the first and last payments and the payment at which principal finally exceeds interest.

Payment Number	Principal	Interest	Balance
1	$81.97	$583.33	$99,918.03
242	$332.97	$332.33	$59,606.38
360	$664.40	$3.88	$00.00

Clearly the lending institution is earning most of its profit in the early years. Since only a small fraction of mortgage holders keep houses for the full thirty years, the lender can collect big interest amounts until there is a sale, at which time the lender gets the principal back and can lend the money again to start earning more profit.

#1 HELPFUL HINT: If you have a computer, it is worth buying an amortization program, which you can use to calculate and show a full schedule of payments for any loan at any rate for any length of time with a few keystrokes (or clicks of a mouse) in a matter of seconds.

See Appendix A, Mortgage/Loan Payment Comparison Table, for monthly payment amounts on 30 year FRMs and 15 year FRMs in different amounts at different interest rates. (See comments about 15 year loans under Combinations and Variations below.)

Adjustable Rate Mortgages

An **A**djustable **R**ate **M**ortgage **(ARM)** starts at a low interest rate (and low monthly payment), and then adjusts upward based on a selected economic indicator (the index), after which the rate follows that indicator up or down. The borrower is gambling that the indicator will remain low; the lender is gambling that it will go up. It's a shared risk.

An ARM might, for example, start at 3.75% and (in timed adjustments) go up to the interest rate for Treasury Bills plus a margin of 2.75%. The result might be 6%, (7%, 8%, 9%, 10%) and stay there until the rate for Treasury Bills changes again.

NOTE: ARMs are not as simple and straightforward as fixed rate loans. As a prospective borrower, you are concerned with several aspects of ARMs (described below) and should check all of them before you accept a loan.

➤ *The Adjustment Period* indicates the frequency of interest rate changes; that is, there can be an adjustment once every six months or once a year (established at the time the loan is written). (A loan with an adjustment period of one year is called a one year ARM.)

➤ *Interest Rate Caps* limit the amount your interest rate can increase. Without caps and with the possibility that the interest rate might go up and up for the life of the loan, ARMs would have much less appeal. The caps go on in two ways.

Periodic Caps limit the interest rate increase from one adjustment period to the next, typically 1% for six-month ARMs or 2% for one-year ARMs.

Overall Lifetime Caps limit the interest rate over the life of the loan. A 10% cap means that the interest rate would never be higher than 10%. Sometimes a cap is established by a start rate. An ARM with a 4.75% start rate and a 6% cap would establish a 10.75% lifetime interest rate cap.

➤ *Payment Caps* limit the amount that the monthly payment can increase at each adjustment time to a percentage of the previous payment. With a 7 1/2% payment cap, for example, a payment of $100 could increase to no more than $107.50 in the first adjustment period and to no more than $115.56 in the second. While ARMs are generally written with rate caps, not all are written with payment caps.

#2

HELPFUL HINT: Consider the length of time you plan to be in your home. An ARM offers certain advantages for short-term residence. If you plan to sell the house within five years, maybe an ARM would work better than an FRM. If your objective is keep the lowest interest rate as long as possible, then maybe an ARM with a payment cap will do the trick even with the possibility -of negative amortization. (More on negative amortization later.)

➤ *The Index* ties ARM interest rate changes to the general movement of interest rates. Lenders use a variety of indexes, including Treasury Bills, Certificates of Deposit, Cost Of Funds (COFI), Prime Rate, London Interbranch Offered Rates (LIBOR), and others. Some lenders use their own indexes based on the performance of their own companies. Some indexes, such as T-Bills, are more volatile than others such as COFI. Your loan agent should be able to tell you how often the index being used changes or how it has behaved in the past. It may be worth your time to examine published reports on indexes in general and the one being used in particular.

➤ *The Margin* is the number of percentage points that lenders add to the index rate to establish the ARM interest rate. The size of the margin represents the lender's profit and varies from one lender to another. Once determined, the margin remains constant throughout the life of the loan. (More on margins later.)

#3 | HELPFUL HINT: Since the margin determines what your future loan payments will be, it is advantageous to find a lender offering a low margin. Do so even if the initial interest rate being offered is higher than most. Remember, your payment will be adjusted, and that initially low interest rate will be short lived.

Sample ARMs

Index rate + margin = new ARM interest rate

$150,000 loan	ARM 1	ARM 2
Initial rate:	3.99%	5.00%
Start payment:	$715.25	$805.23
Margin:	3.25%	2.125%
Index (t-bill):	3.50%	3.50%
Adjustment period:	6 months	1 year
Interest rate adjustment: (margin + index)	6.75%	5.625%
New monthly payment	$972.89	$863.48

9

In this example, an attractive interest rate in ARM 1 would save you $539 in the first 6 months ($805.23 - $715.25 X 6). At the first adjustment, however, the higher margin in ARM 1 would cause it to cost you more. In fact you would actually suffer a net loss of $466 ($972-89 - $805.23 X 6 = $1,005.96 less the $539 saved in the first six months, which means an actual loss of $466.96).

The margin is, therefore, the key to an ARM as seen in ARM 2. Of course, there are other factors to consider such as payment, interest rate, and life caps, but the sample shows that you should look beyond interest rates when considering an ARM.

➤ *Negative Amortization* means that a mortgage balance increases because the monthly payments are not large enough to cover the interest due. That situation occurs when a payment cap is employed. Payment caps limit only the amount of payment increases. Interest rates might go up and call for an adjustment of the monthly payment to an amount higher than the payment cap allows. Payments might not cover all of the interest due on a mortgage (much less apply anything to principal). In its simplest form, if the payment is $50 lower than the interest due, $50 would automatically be added to the balance due , and interest might be charged on that amount. Consider this example:

> The first 12 payments of $570.42 on a $65,000 loan at 10% would pay the balance down to $64,638.72 at the end of the first year. If the rate goes up to 12% in the second year, a payment cap of 7.5% would mean that the payments could increase by only $42.79, which is not high enough to cover all the 12% interest. The interest shortage is added to the debt (with interest on it), which produces a negative amortization of $420.90 during the second year.

Beginning loan amount   *$65,000*

Loan amount @ end of first year = $64,638.72

Negative amortization in the second year =
$420.90

Loan amount @ end of 2nd year =$65,059.62

($64,638.72 + $420.90)

(If you sold your house at this point, you would
owe almost $60.00 more than the amount you
originally borrowed.)

Prepayment Penalties, if written into the agreement, call for assessment of special fees if you pay off an ARM early. (Such a penalty may also be part of an FRM.) Many ARMs allow the borrower to pay the loan in full or in part without penalty whenever the rate is adjusted.

> ➤ *A Conversion Feature* allows the borrower to change the ARM to a fixed rate mortgage at designated times. Such a clause is made a part of the agreement. When you convert, the new rate is generally set at the current market rate for fixed rate mortgages plus a small differential. A convertible ARM may require paying a special fee at the time of conversion. (More on conversion under Convertible Loans in the next section.)

> ➤ *Floors and Ceilings* are also considered minimums and maximums. Ceiling is another name for a lifetime cap. Conversely, a floor is the lowest the interest rate will ever be. This rate is sometimes limited by the beginning note rate or teaser rate.

When you apply for an ARM, your lender is required by law to provide you with a Consumer Handbook On Adjustable Rate Mortgages.

Combinations and Variations

Twenty or Fifteen Year Fixed Rates

While most fixed rate loans are written for 30 years, shorter terms are generally available. For that $100,000 loan at 7% for 15 years, the monthly payment would be approximately $898.93. The amount applied to principal the first month would be almost four times as much as that in the 30 year loan ($315.50 to $81.97). Fifteen year loans usually carry lower interest rates, so let's look at a comparison.

6.5% X $100,000 = $6,500 X 15 years = $97,500 interest
7.5% X $100,000 = $7,500 X 30 years = $225,500 interest ($127,500 more interest)

If your loan is closer to $200,000, that would mean paying about $250,000 more in interest over the life of the loan. Thus, if your plans call for paying off a mortgage more quickly and if you wish to decrease the amount of interest paid, the shorter-term loan has a clear advantage. The chief disadvantage for most borrowers is that the monthly payment on a 15-year loan is higher.

#4

HELPFUL HINT: If your objective is to pay off a loan early and pay less interest, the arithmetic may be better if you take the 30 year loan and pay more than required each month. Your payment coupon or statement may already have a space for indicating added principal; if not, write it. If you make one additional payment each year, you could pay off the loan in roughly 18 years.

Thirty Due in Five (or Three or Seven)

You may be able to get a loan that is written as a regular 30 year loan but that requires payment of the full balance at the end of three or five or seven years. Such a loan abbreviated to 30/3, 30/5, or 3/7-is called, quite graphically, a "balloon" loan. It might offer a lower interest rate (and monthly payment) and would

11

be advantageous if you plan to sell within that time.

You may also be able to get a rollover feature that allows changing the loan to a full 30 year loan (at prevailing rates) at the end of five or seven years, probably with the payment of some fee. Given that, your loan would begin at say 7% for the first 5 years, then make a one-time adjustment to 9% for the next 25 years. The shorthand becomes 5/25 or 7/23. If you don't sell or rollover and don't have a trunk full of cash, you'll have to refinance and go through the mortgage maze again.

Convertible Loans

It may be a misnomer to speak of a "convertible loan" instead of an "ARM with a conversion feature," but the term "convertible loan" is used and is, therefore, included here. As was noted earlier, the conversion feature becomes part of ARM agreement, usually at some cost to the borrower, and establishes a window, usually the thirteenth to sixtieth month, during which time the borrower can convert the ARM to an FRM. A fee is ordinarily assessed at the time of conversion. The new fixed rate is not set at prevailing rates but at the then current rate plus a small margin.

12

The prospect that you could get an ARM at some very, very low rate for a year or two, maybe longer, then convert to a very low FRM before rates start to rise may seem quite attractive. If, however, fixed rates are not attractive during the window of opportunity, you could be paying for something that you will never use. Before you choose that feature, consider four points very carefully:

1) **when the loan can be converted,**
2) **what the feature costs up front,**
3) **what it costs at the time of conversion**
4) **what the new fixed rate will be.**

#5 HELPFUL HINT: Before you make a decision concerning the conversion feature, run the arithmetic several ways. Figure cost of payments during each adjustment period for the length of time the window is open. Project what the fixed rate might be at various times. Factor in your financial situation and the probable time you'll keep the property. Then decide.

Advertised Specials

The loans that you hear and see advertised are not really kinds of loans, but they should be mentioned. A no-point (or zero point) loan is one, which does not require the borrower to pay a loan origination fee. A no-fee (or zero fee) loan is one that does not require paying of fees normally assessed by the lending institution-title, escrow,appraisal, credit, and the like. With all such loans, you need to know what charges will be assessed-not what will not be assessed. Dropped fees can be replaced by other fees. (More on the subject at the end of the Getting Technical on Rates section.)

NOTE: There is no such thing as a free loan. The lending institution will charge you for making the loan. Those costs may be paid out of pocket by you, or they may be added to the principal of the loan (which means that you will be paying interest on those charges), but you will pay to get a loan.

13

#6 HELPFUL HINT: Always remind yourself that a 30 or 60 second ad on radio or a 2" x 1" ad in a newspaper is only a tease. A full description of all the terms of a loan which you must have-requires much more time or space. The ads can't be entirely deceptive, but do notice such practices as putting the words "NO POINTS" in big print and under that the word "available" in small print. You pay in some way other than points for that loan.

Loan Limits

Various entities set limits on loans. The Veteran's Administration has a maximum beyond which it will not guarantee the loan. Loans may be termed "conventional" or "jumbo." In the 1990s in California, the conventional loan has been limited to a figure just above $200,000. Any loan above the conventional is a jumbo, generally carries a higher interest rate, and requires stronger evidence of ability to pay. Since this book was written in the 1980's, it's highly probable that the loan amounts, which establish conventional/conforming and Jumbo limits, have increased. A quick visit to your local lender or a newspaper will confirm new limits.

Getting Technical on Rates

The complexity of the mortgage business has been noted. The following information on pricing sheets and rates can provide you with some understanding of ways that charges are established and applied. Even if the details are too technical for full absorption, you can get the idea.

Every day, thousands of interest rates are offered by thousands of private investors, banks, insurance companies, and pension funds. It is the job of lending agents to identify the best programs relative to price (points) and interest rate for their clients' needs. Clients are generally given one price: 4.5% plus 1 point, for example. Lending agents and brokers, however, see pricing sheets with technical details from which they can give you choices of the way that you want your loan set up. In the following example of price offerings for ARMs, you see across the top line the margins that were referred to earlier. Again, a margin is the lending institution's acceptable profit expectation and is added to the stated index to calculate payments at each adjustment period. Below the margins in the first column on the left are interest rates. Rebates from the lender and points to the lender are shown in the other columns.

Read across the interest rate rows and down the margin column. This simple chart shows 54 combinations, 54 possible prices for a loan. (We'll get to the 10 and 22 day points in a moment.)

Lenders work with hundreds of money sources. When you consider that each source has its own pricing strategy and each product has its own combination of pricing options, you begin to appreciate the number of pricing options available to a lender. After all, 54 X a lot = a whole lot of options.

Margin	2.625		2.375		2.125	
	Points		Points		Points	
Rate	10 day	22 day	10 day	22 day	10 day	22 day
4.875% @	(3.625	(3.500)	(3.000)	(2.875)	(2.375)	(2.250)
4.750% @	(3.250)	(3.125)	(2.625)	(2.500)	(2.125)	(2.000)
4.625% @	(3.000)	(2.875)	(2.375)	(2.260)	(1.750)	(1.625)
4.500% @	(2.500)	(2.375)	(2.000)	(1.875)	(1.500)	(1.375)
4.375% @	(2.250)	(2.125)	(1.625)	(1.500)	(1.125)	(1.000)
4.250% @	(1.625)	(1.500)	(1.125)	(1.000)	(0.625)	(0.500)
4.125% @	(1.125)	(1.000)	(0.625)	(0.500)	(0.125)	**0.000**
4.000% @	(0.625)	(0.500)	(0.250)	(0.125)	0.2500	.375
3.875% @	(0.250)	(0.125)	0.2500	.3750	.7500	.875

The points figures in parentheses are rebates, fees that a lender or investor pays to a lending agent for selling its loans. In addition, a rebate is generally given when a lending agent sells a loan at a price higher than the going market; it's an incentive to the agent.

The lower the margin, the better for you as a borrower. A lower margin, however, means less profit for the lender. So as the margins decline from 2.625% to 2.125%, the cost to you increases or the incentive to the lending agent decreases.

All that may be a bit confusing. Perhaps the example that follows will clarify.

Look at the last column on the right. Notice that these prices are for an ARM with a very attractive margin of 2.125%. Now, find the points that correspond to a 4.125% interest rate. You see that the cost to the agent by the lender is 0.000 points. (When money costs 0.000 points that is known as "par.") If a broker gives you a loan at par pricing, that broker would make no immediate income on that loan.

15

Notice that as interest rates increase, the incentive in the brackets increases. Thus, at 4.25%, the broker would receive .50% but at 4.375% would receive 1.00%. If, however, you as a client want the lowest interest rate possible, then a broker would give you a rate of 3.875%. That sounds good to you but not to the broker because to give you that rate, the broker would have to pay .875% to the lender. The broker would lose money on that loan, so since you want the rate, you pay the .875%. That sounds reasonable, but the broker still needs to make a living and will, therefore, increase the cost to you. The broker may charge you 1.875%, with .875% for the interest rate charged by the lender and the other 1.00% as the broker's profit.

If you are more interested in lower cost for the loan than in the lowest interest rate, you may be offered a rate of 4.375%, which allows the agent to collect the same profit of 1.00% directly from the lender and not from you. The trade off is simple. The higher the interest rate, the greater the return for the broker. The lower the rate, the higher the cost to the agent and ultimately to you.

Now, to the 10 and 22 days columns: they address the time for locking the interest rate. (Locking rates will be discussed later, but briefly locking a rate is an agreement between lender and borrower that the interest rate will be guaranteed for a certain period of time.)

Since the job of lenders and investors is to move as much money as possible through the credit system, they pay incentives to get loans completed at a quicker pace. The quicker some amount of money funds a particular loan, the faster the investment can show profits. The longer the process takes, the greater the loss of profits and the greater the chance that lending opportunities will be missed.

A broker or lending agent is, therefore, given a slight pricing advantage if he is able to deliver an active, closed, performing loan. Once a rate has been locked, an agent wants to sell it to the open market. Go back to the rate chart, and you'll see that the incentive is greater for a 10 day turnaround than for a 22 day turnaround. Locks and delivery dates come in a variety of different intervals. Your concern, as a borrower, may not be the same as that of the agent. If interest rates are rising, then you want to lock your rate near the beginning of the process. You may wish to pay the price of a 60 day lock to reduce the risk that by the time your loan is processed you'll be liable for a significantly higher interest rate. Conversely, if the market rates are declining, then it is best to wait as long as you can for the fall to continue before you lock your interest rate (or you may never lock a rate). Hence, the best incentives are on short-term locks.

We covered a lot of area, so take a moment to review the rate sheet. You should now be familiar with the relationship between higher rates and higher incentives and between lower rates and higher costs. You should note that pricing incentives are offered on short-term locks over longer lock periods.

Here's one last concept. In the flurry of refinancing in the late 1980's, zero point and zero fee loans became hot items in many markets. Who knows, they might come back in the future and so we should discuss further. The ads made it sound as if lending institutions were having a huge sale on money and were lowering their prices out of the goodness of their hearts. The question is: "What do zero points and zero fees mean when it is time to crunch the numbers and write the loan?" As an example, let's say that a loan amount of $272,000 would carry a cost of $5,110, which includes a 1 % profit return for the broker. Given those amounts, a broker under the 2.375% margin 22-day lock would have to offer an interest rate of 4.5%. The rebate would give the broker enough money to pay for the closing cost on your behalf and maintain that 1% return for profit. But there's a red flag. What if the broker tells you that he has obtained a zero point, zero fee loan for you at a rate of 4.875%? That would mean that you got what you wanted, and he got a healthy return above that which he expected.

His rebate would then be 2.875%.

Multiply $272,000 X 2.875%, and the rebate would be $7,820.

Subtract $5,110 (cost plus profit), and the broker would have $2,710 extra profit.

Add that $2,710 to $2,720 (the existing 1 point profit),

The new broker profit is $5,430.

The broker would actually receive 2% instead of 1 point.

All on a zero point, zero fee loan?

Everyone wins. Right? Maybe not when you consider that his greed would prevent you from obtaining a better interest rate. There is nothing illegal about this, but you are not getting the best deal for your money. You should ask questions about the cost of the loan, including the rebate. If you feel that the return to the broker is unreasonable, ask him to reconsider his cost. Don't be unreasonable, however; the services of a good broker are worth more than some savings.

Remember: It is important to look beyond interest rates.

Continuing Your Research

The information given thus far should get you thinking in ways that will make your first steps into the mortgage maze much more certain than if you blindly stepped in. There are, of course, volumes of information available on mortgages. A trip to a library or database can let you see just how many books there are. One way to get an idea of what books are out there is to go to the reference section of a library or to a bookstore or on-line and ask to see the *Subject Guide to Books in Print.*

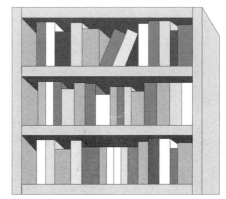

Don't let the number of books overwhelm you. In the first place, many of them contain essentially the same information. In the second place, many of them are written for people in the mortgage business and not for consumers; unless you already have training or experience, you'll find the material more technical than you need or want.

Do read newspaper and magazine articles. No book, including this one, which takes more time to prepare and print than an article, can provide the most current information and practices the way newspapers and

17

magazines can. And no book can give you local rules and practices, as can newspapers and magazines.

#7 | **HELPFUL HINT**: Your gathering of information can and should continue. Set up a file or a drawer or a box for mortgage materials. If you collect enough, you may need to arrange the materials by topics and use several files folders for one topic.

Getting necessary information—and understanding that information-will enable you to avoid costly mistakes and stay on the right path through the mortgage maze.

➤ *A critical part of getting information is asking questions. If an answer does not tell you what you want to know, you may not have asked the right question. Try again.*

➤ *The test of your understanding is being able to re-state information. Make it a habit to say: "Now, let me see whether I have that right."*

18

#8 | HELPFUL HINT: In addition to marking and noting information in this book, put information that you gather from other sources in writing while it is still fresh in your mind. Include date, place, and source of information.

Sharing usable information was a primary purpose for the writing of this book. Taking that information and making good use of it are your purposes for studying this book. Keep those purposes in mind, ask questions, and verify your understanding, and you should stay on the right path all the way through the mortgage maze.

Chapter Two

A Companion for the Trip:

Choosing a Loan Agent

As you start this chapter and get closer to entering the mortgage maze, I trust that you are keeping before you two points: first, asking about interest rates alone does not produce the answers you need, and, second, you should know what you do need and what you want to do with your money and your property.

Framing Your Questions

There is no reason not to call a few lenders to get the feel of what is out there, but before you get involved with or make any commitment to anyone, make a list of the things that you want and need to know. Before you can make any comparisons, you should at least know:

➤ How much: a particular loan will cost you.......

> how much it will cost out-of-pocket
> how much it will add to the principal
> how much it will add to monthly payments
> how much it will add during the life of the loan
> how much it will cost to lock a rate

➤ How much the monthly payment will be at sample interest rates

➤ What happens when anything changes, such as sale of the property, end of a set five or seven year period, or a rate adjustment.

To those points, add others that stand out in your assessment of your needs. It will not be easy to get all that information. It will not be possible to get it in a two-minute telephone call. If, however, a lending agent cannot or will not put information in your terms, perhaps that person is not the one for you.

Looking at the Lenders

At one time, the title of this chapter would have been Choosing a Lender because the lenders were almost exclusively banks or S&L's, and the borrower went to one of those and dealt with an available loan officer. If you look in the Yellow Pages today, you'll find a few banks and a few savings banks among many mortgage or financial companies. As the Internet becomes more discussed as the wave of the future, who knows how many more lending options will be made available to consumers.

If you look through various sections of your newspaper, you'll find small ads, big ads all promising the best loans. If you have bought or sold a house recently or taken a home equity loan or done anything else that could get your name on a mailing list, you have received ads in the mail-all promising the best loans. And you've probably found flyers at your door with the same promise. By the time that you checked even ten or twenty of them, the first ones would have new or different loans available. The size of the city or town in which you live, of course, determines the number of places you can go, but if you live far from a town or city, you can get your mortgage by mail or maybe someday by computer.

There are hundreds of established lenders who pull money from various sources and make that money available for real estate loans. Some of those lenders may make loans directly available to home buyers. Most of them provide funds to the entities listed below, which in turn write mortgage loans for home buyers. To people in the world of finance-the professionals and the investors-the mortgage loan business is fascinating and exciting. To other people, it is mysterious and secretive-and perhaps suspect. You may want to concern yourself with such matters another time. Right now, you are concerned with getting the best mortgage loan possible, which means that you will be looking at the possibilities and approaches discussed in the rest of this chapter.

Banks and Savings Banks

In a growing economy there are more banks and more branches. In a shrinking economy there are fewer. The big banks-Bank of America in California, Chase Manhattan and, of course, Citicorp in New York-are still there. Some local banks, community banks, have been in business for decades (a few survived the depression and all the changes since then); they must be doing something right. The former S&L's, the ones that survived and became savings banks and are showing strength, provide adequate service. Those institutions have loan officers sitting at desks to take your calls and process your loan. Some of those loan officers go to the homes or businesses of customers to take applications. Some work outside usual business hours.

The loan officers can offer you whatever packages the institution has available. The number of those packages varies: some institutions may have one or two FRMs and one or two ARMs. Others may offer a wide range of loans from their own offices and may also handle VA, FHA, or retirement system loans or other loans not generally available. Some may be highly competitive; some may not.

SAVINGS & LOAN

21

If you have done most of your business with one of those institutions across many years, if you have been pleased with the service, system, and staff, if staff members know you and seem to have your interests at heart, and if you know that fees and rates are not out of line, then you can save time and gain satisfaction by continuing to use that bank.

Thrift and Loan Associations

Thrift and Loans generally offer loans on a short-term basis and at higher rates because they primarily handle loans that are difficult to process or approve. They are a good source for commercial, construction, or junior liens such as second and third mortgages. They are similar to S&L's in that they take in deposits and lend on those deposits. They are, however, governed by different operating laws.

Credit Unions

Credit unions have only recently begun offering real estate loans. 'The kinds of loans offered are probably limited. If so, members are often referred to a local broker which has formed an agreement with the credit union. There is an advantage in working with an institution that serves only its members. The question is whether your credit union competes favorably with the kind of loan you want or offers only one or two kinds of loans. Closing costs are generally minimal to members.

Mortgage Bankers and Mortgage Brokers

While mortgage bankers have been around for years, the number of companies has recently increased; the number of agents working with mortgage companies has increased; and the number of independent brokers has increased.

Brokers take loan applications, process the loans, and see the loans closed-the same things that a loan officer at a bank would do. There are differences, however. Loan officers at banks work with the money supply and rates of the bank. Brokers work with the money supply and rates of any lender with whom they have established a working relationship, including mortgage bankers, banks, S&L's, credit unions, thrift companies, insurance companies, pension funds, and private investors.

As a one time loan broker and owner of a mortgage company, I, quite naturally, think that the prospective borrower will be well (even best) served by a broker-a good broker, that is. I know that many people don't like the idea of using brokers of any kind. Stock brokers have come in for quite a bit of criticism in the last few years, and, I have to admit, some loan brokers are greedy or incompetent or both. The image has been created that brokers are unnecessary "middlemen" who make money at everybody else's expense. I also know that even more people are not quite sure what a broker is. Let me explain.

In the world of real estate, lenders have money to lend, money on which they wish to make a profit. Those lenders generally are not set up to receive and process applications from individuals. Individuals want to buy houses or refinance existing loans. They are faced with the prospect of studying financing and lending, evaluating lenders, and processing loans.

The broker can save the lender time and money by pulling together everything that the lender wants to know about the individual and the property. (The very number of brokers means that the lender automatically reaches many, many more people.)

The broker can save the borrower time and money by pulling everything together for the borrower and presenting it in the best possible package to the best matched lender (or lenders) and thereby increase the likelihood that the lender will approve the loan.

The broker serves both lender and borrower by seeing that all details, all forms, all requirements are taken care of. The money the broker earns is the money that the lender and the borrower save in the process.

Let me be even more partial to using brokers for just a moment. If you apply for a loan at a bank, you will pay about $50 for a credit report and $250 to $500 for an appraisal (and perhaps an application fee). At those prices, you can't afford to apply at two or three banks at the same time to increase your chances for getting a loan. (Competing banks don't share information; each wants to use its own sources.) If you wait weeks, and a bank turns you down, you have lost a great deal of time and money and have to start all over with another institution, where you may lose more money and time.

That's not likely to happen if you use a seasoned and well-informed broker. An independent broker may deal with 150 or more lenders. That broker, using the same application, the same credit report, and the same appraisal, can put your request before many lenders not just one. In fact, there are "niche lenders," lenders who prefer to make loans on particular kinds of property or to certain categories of customers, and the loan broker will present your application to the best matched lender first.

Because of that flexibility, a loan broker can make more loan options available. If you are on your way to a fixed rate loan with lender "A" and conclude that an ARM would be better for you, and lender "B" is offering a better ARM than lender "A", the loan broker can move everything to lender "B" without additional expense of time or money.

Finding the Lending Agent for You

In many ways, the person with whom you work is more important than the company or institution. In fact, you may find in one institution the best and the worst.

Here is one borrower's story:

I was in a partnership on a couple of properties. I checked out about six banks for one loan. Two banks said no, two banks said yes, and two banks never said. One of the two that said yes offered a lower interest rate, no prepayment penalties, and some other advantages, so I chose to go with bank A. The lending officer from bank B wished me well and said she would keep in touch. A week later, she called, asked a few questions, and told me that she had ordered a drive-by appraisal and that the property was worth more than the requested loan. When I protested that I hadn't authorized anything, she assured me that I was incurring no obligation and added that she was just keeping things moving so that I wouldn't lose time in case things didn't work out with bank A.

Truth is that things weren't working out with bank A. I could never get my agent by telephone, and she seldom returned my calls the same day. When it came time for my partners to make full applications, she said they would have to make an appointment and drive (some distance) during her business hours to give her information and to sign the necessary forms.

The agent from bank B continued to call, and we were talking like old friends. I told her that my partners were going to have to take time off from work and drive to the other bank. She said that she would be glad to drive to my partners' workplaces and meet them at lunchtime or any other time. When she found a way to shave a quarter of a percent off the interest rate, I switched from A to B and was well pleased that I did.

A year or two later, when we were going to buy the second house, we went to another branch of bank B because my partners had current applications on file there. The agent there had my partners complete new applications anyway. She said she could get a loan for me through a retirement program but never did. The answers I got when I called the retirement offices indicated that she hadn't called. When I pressed for action, she got angry. When I wanted one of the bank's advertised loans-the one that worked best for us-she said, "Oh no, You don't want that. This other one is better." After a week or two of nothing but annoyed responses that she hadn't had time to do something, or I hadn't done what I was supposed to, I picked up all our materials and asked for a refund of fees I had paid. We lost something over a month of loan processing time.

You deserve to have a mortgage professional like the first one from bank B, not one of the other two. You are, in effect, baring your financial soul to your loan agent; you want mutual trust and understanding. (Yes, perhaps if you know full well what you are doing, you can make certain that the agent does what you want done and can therefore work with anyone, but that's not ideal.)

As you start your search, here are some points to consider so that you aren't lured into the mortgage maze by a promise of fast action and low rates and then discover your guide isn't going to get you through to the loan you want. (Some of the points are related primarily to loan officers in institutions, some primarily to loan brokers, and some to either.)

Learning from Others Who've Been through the Maze

➤   Talk to as many people as possible about their experiences.

➤   Some people like to talk; some don't. Some think of mortgage information as facts of life to be shared; some consider money matters private and personal. Proceed accordingly.

➤   Be aware that some people like to complain (and will make their experiences sound worse than they were), and some people don't like to say they lost or made mistakes (and will put a good face on any experience).

➤   You can evaluate responses of people you know with greater accuracy than those of people you don't know.

➤   Ask about the company and the agent. Use the examples below to formulate your set of questions.

➤   **Ask specific, concrete questions**

What rate were you quoted going in?

What rate did you get?

How closely did the Good Faith Estimate of the cost of the loan come to the actual charges that you paid?

How much time elapsed from application to closing?

Did you have to submit more documentation during processing? Why?

25

Were any documents lost or misplaced?

Were you asked to switch to a different loan?

Were you told that the loan you requested was no longer available?

What did it cost to lock your rate?

Responses to such questions give you concrete information that is far more usable than questions that call for general, abstract, or judgmental responses. Questions of those kinds have some value and should also be asked; indeed, it might be easier to get people to talk with you if you ask some of those questions first. Some examples:

Were you pleased with the way your loan was handled?

Was the processing efficient?

Did you feel good when you signed that last document at closing?

If you were starting another loan tomorrow, would you go back to that company?

Would you go back happily or reluctantly?

➤ Rely on your memory long enough to make notes of information and sources after you talk with someone (taking notes while you are talking can be distracting). Do not rely on your memory for keeping a tally of the number of favorable and unfavorable responses given about a bank or of what five people said about rates or time required to fund a loan. To see a clear picture of what you have learned, make a chart.

➤ Read accounts in newspapers and magazines. Work that information into your chart.

<u>Looking at Companies and Institutions</u>

➤ Consider the length of time a company or institution has been in business, its general reputation, and the number of loans of the kind you want that it has made.

➤ Consider what support (including staff and office operations) the company or institution provides for the loan agent. Ask about other persons with whom you will interact.

➤ Ask officers of the company or institution about such matters. Ask for references and then ask those people about their experiences with obtaining a mortgage there. Ask any other people you can contact for their opinions.

➤ Ask about appraisers used and appraisal fees, about escrow companies used and escrow fees, and about title companies used and title fees.

➤ Ask those other real estate professionals-appraisers, escrow companies, title companies-about working with the company or institution in question and ask what they would charge you for their services if you had private funding.

➤ You might be able to get lower prices on those services than a lending company offers you. On the other hand, you may discover that some lending companies get major discounts (wholesale prices), perhaps paying as little as $350 for an escrow that would cost you $800.

➤ Ask banks and particularly mortgage brokers whether they are approved to conduct business with the best investors and funding sources. Ask for the names of investors and funding sources used. Some of the companies should sound familiar to you. If not, ask more questions.

➤ Many investors have retail direct-to-the-public operations and may assess lower fees. On the other hand, wholesale brokers may run their businesses with low overhead, and at the same time investors may offer them lower rates and fees to get more of their volume of business.

➤ Investors have broker approval processes, some of them quite strict, through which brokers must go before being authorized to sell loans. Again, ask your broker the names of investors the company has been approved to do business with.

➤ Ask what mortgage products or programs are available. Many companies are quite limited. You may be satisfied with a company that offers only some specific loan, but generally you're better off if the company has a variety of fixed and adjustable rate loans, offers short term and long term loans, has experience with first time buyers, high income borrowers, self-employed borrowers, and so on.

27

➤ If a lender offers only a 30 year FRM on $150,000 at 7%, your payment would be $997 per month. If another lender offers a loan that runs for five years at 6.5% with a payment of $948 and you plan to keep your property only five years, you want that loan. Over the five year period that difference of $49 a month would cost you $2,940 at the 7% rate.

Getting a Picture of Loan Officers and Agents

While you're asking about companies, ask about the person you'll be working with.

Ask specific questions:

➤ Did the officer/agent return your calls in a timely manner?

➤ Did the officer/agent remember you and your proper ty and some details from call to call?

➤ Did the officer/agent ask for the same information repeatedly?

➤ Did the officer/agent seem to understand what you said?

➤ Did the officer/agent answer questions in ways that made sense and that you understood?

➤ Did the officer/agent prepare you for things to come or spring surprises?

➤ Was the officer/agent cordial and cooperative?

➤ Was the officer/agent efficient and effective?

➤ Were you comfortable with the officer/agent throughout the process?

➤ What did you think of your officer/agent as you were signing your name hundreds of times for the closing officer? Were you complimentary to your agent, or did you find yourself blaming the closing officer for what your agent did or didn't do?

➤ Would you recommend the officer/agent to your very best friend?

➤ Talk to the officer/agent more than once:

➤ Ask about the officer/agent's work; be interested in the officer/agent.

➤ Ask about trends in the mortgage business.

➤ Ask about the way the officer/agent's company processes a loan.

➤ Ask how many mortgage loans the officer/agent has written.

➤ Ask for references.

➤ Observe whether the officer/agent focuses on you-even while doing other things.

➤ Consider the kinds of answers you get to your questions.

➤ Repeat questions if the answers are not clear.

➤ Ask yourself whether you feel comfortable and confident with the officer/agent.

<u>Making Your Decision</u>

You won't get full and complete information on all of the items named. You may not have the time, and other people may not be willing to give you that much time. You will, however, get more than you might expect to get.

#9

HELPFUL HINT: Whenever you find yourself saying, "They're all alike. What does it matter?" remember that borrowers seldom start the process all over with a new lender-no matter how unhappy, no matter how far from the loan they wanted. It's simply easier to continue than to start again with someone else-even if the idea loan agent miraculously appeared.

You can't continue the process indefinitely if you want to get a mortgage. I don't know who should get credit for the expression, "paralysis of analysis," but it is a very apt expression. There will always be just one more person you want to talk with, just one more fact you want to check. At some point, you have to say, "Enough," and use the information that you have to make a decision.

> ➢ Lay out all the information you have.

> ➢ Weigh it.

> ➢ Discuss it with spouse, partners, friends.

> ➢ Compare people and businesses.

> ➢ Compare like things: APR to APR or cost to cost; don't put rates against points.

> ➢ Rank people and businesses.

> ➢ Check your gut response; add that to the ranking.

> ➢ Make your choice and get to work.

Chapter Three

A Road Map for the Trip:

Completing the Application

As you talk with the person who will be your loan representative (even before you've decided to use that person), you will be discussing your needs and options. A good loan representative starts interviewing you with the first contact. When you say, "O.K., let's get started," you and he/she will schedule a full interview and get more specific about where you're going and how you're going to get there.

The job of the loan agent is to get you through the mortgage maze to your loan. If you'd prefer to think in terms of taking a trip, your loan agent is your tour guide, one who knows all about the place you want to go and the best way to get there. The agent will take important information such as your employment history, credit history, and mortgage needs and create a map and an itinerary.

All that information will make a thick file before you're through. Lenders seem to want more and more documentation of almost everything.

The lead item in that file will be your loan application. You can wait until you get the specific form you'll use, or, while you're still looking for a loan agent or a lender, you can start pulling together your entire financial history-**and that means borrower and co-borrower: spouse, partner, other relative, anyone whose name will be on the mortgage.**

Pulling Your Information Together

Unless you are so well organized that you can immediately produce every document, every deed, every account number, full records of payments, tax records, and a dozen other such pieces of paper, you'll look at the application, groan, and then find yourself digging through drawers and boxes, writing and telephoning for information, and using the strongest language you ever use. And be forewarned: no matter how much information you provide, the lender is going to want more.

Some lenders have their house form, which must be used. Many lenders today use the Uniform Residential Loan Application, which will be shown and discussed in the next step, "Filling Out That Form." Copies of the form are readily available if you'd like to work with the actual form, or you can use the sample form that follows-and the discussion as a guide for gathering information.

32

#10 | HELPFUL HINT: Keep in mind that a lender wants to know that you can pay and that you will pay. You want to show adequate income and a good record of payments.

A list of the kinds of things you'll need follows. The application form you are given may not call for all the items, but if you're on the borderline for qualifying for the loan, you'll be relieved and pleased when you're asked for additional documentation and can say, "Oh, that's right here." In fact, you'll almost wish the loan agent would ask for something else.

#11 | HELPFUL HINT: Set up separate file folders for 1.) Tax returns, 2.) Income (subdivide if you have multiple sources of income), 3.) Debts, 4.) Real estate now owned, 5.) Real estate now buying, 6.) Records of payments (check registers, at least), and 7.) Other categories that your situation calls for. Include more pay stubs and such than called for. You'll save yourself time later, and you'll make your loan agent very happy.

➤ Tax Returns

Almost everyone will need at least the last two years' federal tax returns. If you are self-employed or run a business, include a current profit and loss statement.

#12

HELPFUL HINT: If your tax returns are very thick, be certain that the pages are numbered, then remove the staples, punch holes, and put each year's return in a loose-leaf notebook. You'll make all handling, especially photocopying, much easier. Be sure that W-2s, 1099s, and other forms stay in place.

➤ Documentation of Primary Income

if you're salaried, you'll need
__those tax returns and W-2 forms
__your last two (or three or four) pay stubs.

If you work on commission, you'll need
__the tax returns,
__your last two years' 1099 forms.

If you're self-employed or own your own business, you'll need those tax returns,
__probably your most recent year-to-date profit and loss statement,
__probably a balance sheet prepared and signed by your accountant,
__and probably a net worth of business statement, listing equipment, inventory, etc.

If you're retired, you'll need
__those tax returns,
—your award letter from your retirement system (Social Security, teachers, etc.),
__check stubs,
__and maybe a statement of vested interest in the retirement system.

➤ Documentation of Other Income

If you receive interest income or investment dividends, you'll need
__those tax returns
__your 1099 forms,

33

__stock certificates, broker's statements, and such.

If you own rental property, you'll need
__those tax returns
__and rental agreements.

If you have income from any other source (part-time employment, gifts, etc.), you'll need similar documentation if you want the income to count toward qualifying you for a loan.

> NOTE: You never have to declare alimony or child support income. If you do, however, you will need to show a divorce decree to prove the history and continued receipt of the income.

About this time you may be asking about those easy qualifying loans, which omit the need for income documentation and instead rely on the borrower's liquid assets. Although EQ loans are still available, they have been linked to the increase in delinquent loans and may well be eliminated in the near future. This guidebook, therefore, does not deal with that option. However, know that they generally require solid credit and are generally at a lower Loan-to Value simply due to risk. They also often are not available to people with salaried income and are designed generally for people with hard to qualify income such as the self-employed. To that, even the self-employed must provide bank statements supporting adequate cash flow in order to confirm that they can carry the payments of the new debt.

➢ Credit History

You'll need all the information on everything you owe. It might be simplest to make a chart, something like this:

Institution Name, Address, Etc.	Kind of Account and Account Number	Credit Limit or Highest Amount Owed	Current Balance	Monthly Payment

#13 | HELPFUL HINT: It may be a good idea for you to get a copy of your credit report before you apply for a loan. The report could help you identify (and do something about) problems (see next helpful hint), and you can be sure that you are not omitting anything–which a lender might assume is something you're trying to hide.

You will be asked about bankruptcies, foreclosures, lawsuits, judgments against you, delinquencies, and any other obligations and liabilities (child support payments,being co-signer on someone else's loan). If there is any thing of such nature in your credit history (now or in the last seven years), do say so. You might be able to overcome derogatory reports, but you can't hide them. Besides, you're signing a declaration that your application is true and that you realize that criminal penalties could be imposed for any misrepresentation.

Be up front with your loan agent. Explain any such matters and ask about the best ways to handle them.

#14 | HELPFUL HINT There may be derogatory comments-which are referred to as "derogs" on your credit report. If you have several derogs, you may be subject to a higher fee and/or interest rate. Removing even one derog may keep you in a favorable position. A quick letter to a creditor regarding a dispute is sometimes all it takes to remove a negative rating or comment. Most creditors offer borrowers a courtesy late payment wavier.

Knowing your credit status early may allow you to remove a derogatory comment. If you have a late payment on your record, call the creditor.

➢ Records of Payments

For the most part, you will not be required to provide detailed records of payments on cars, credit cards, and such because that information appears on your credit report. You may, however, be asked when you paid your taxes or fire insurance or something else so you should be prepared to provide a date or check number or receipt.

Sometimes, something more is needed. If two partners own a property, and one of them makes all the payments, the paying partner may need proof that the payments were made, and the other may need the same proof to show that the payments are not a monthly obligation. It may then be necessary to produce cancelled checks (or to order copies if the bank uses checks with copies beneath and does not return cancelled checks). Bank statements showing that a check in the amount of the payment has cleared each month might suffice.

➤ Checking and Savings Accounts Statements

You'll need your last two or three statements for each account to give a picture of your monthly money.

If you are making a down payment from cash on hand or from savings, you'll need to show that you didn't just acquire the money.

If you have several accounts, make a chart showing addresses, kind of accounts, account numbers, and balances.

➤ Source of Down Payment

Lenders want to know that you are not borrowing a down payment from your brother-in-law and thereby obligating yourself for an additional monthly payment that won't show on a credit report and which might increase your debt to income ratio enough to disqualify you. You will, therefore, have to show the source of the down payment.

If you are selling other property to obtain the down payment, you'll need a copy of the escrow instructions, the sales contract, and an estimated closing statement prepared by the settlement agent.

By the way, it's all right to make the down payment with a gift; just be certain that you disclose the information to your loan agent.

➤ Real Estate You Own

Whether you own one house or two or three or an office building or vacant land, for each property you'll need the address of the property, the kind of property, present market value (your estimate or someone else's), purchase price, amount of mortgages and liens, mortgage payments, home owner's association dues, taxes, insurance, maintenance costs, and gross and net rental income. If you have several properties, make a chart to include at least the items shown. For a full and complete chart, see Appendix B, Schedule of Real Estate Owned.

Property Address	Type	Value	Mortgage	*	Mortgage Payments	Insurance Taxes, etc.	**

*If you have rental income, include a column for that here and a column for net rental income at the right side (**).

Have grant deeds, title insurance, and other legal documents available.

➤ Real Estate You're Buying

You'll need your sales contract and escrow instructions. Unless this is a different property from the one for which you are now seeking a loan, your loan agent will work directly with realty and escrow companies.

➤ Listing of Other Assets

Include everything: cars, trucks, stocks, bonds, furniture, household items, electrical and electronic items (including tools, appliances, television set, VCR, stereo sets, computer), art, antiques, and jewelry.... You won't be asked for the list, but you will be asked for an amount. Unless you have made a complete inventory, you will probably underestimate the value of your personal property.

#15 HELPFUL HINT: After your loan is closed, you're enjoying your good loan, and you have your fingers on more of your records than usual, get a homeowners inventory form from your insurance agent and start your own inventory. You'll be quite surprised at the number of things you own. If you really want to do it right, you'll record everything on paper and with a video camera; then you'll send one copy of each to your insurance agent and put another in a safe deposit box. You'll have a good record if you ever need it, and you'll have done something that many of us think about but that few of us ever do-or only do after a serious loss.

37

Although you may be asked for other pieces of information, those listed are the main ones-the ones to have ready and in good order.

#16 | HELPFUL HINT: Once you get all that information together, file or store it in some specific place that will let you get it again easily. A special box with everything neatly arranged and ordered is ideal. (Just remember where you put the box.) You'll be very pleased with yourself when some new development calls for some or all of it.

Filling Out That Form

For some people, filling out forms is a clear and simple process; for others, the headings and the blank spaces never match their particular information. Fortunately, your loan agent will prepare the final form whether it's from the application form you filled out or from other sheets that contain all the information. **Please note:** your loan agent cannot make up information for you (and could go to jail for doing so), and an incomplete application won't go anywhere.

Any loan agent who wants applications to be approved is going to get applications on a computer so that changes can be made easily and new copies (originals, actually) can be printed quickly.

The loan agent can go to your home or office, or you can go to the agent's office. If you go to the agent, the agent's support staff can photocopy your documents and return them to you immediately. If the agent goes to you, you'll either have to make photocopies of all the required documents or allow the agent to take them for copying and return.

#17 | HELPFUL HINT: Documents do get lost. Know where your original documents are stored, and do not ever give away any original documents. Do provide good, clear photocopies on good paper.

The loan agents call it "taking an app," but it's also a loan interview- an hour-long conference, actually-during which the agent will more definitely and specifically determine your situation, your needs, and your desires. Your agent will lay out options and make suggestions. As you go through the application together, everything will be more tightly focused. You'll be able to make choices at that time, or you might decide to make some of the choices later.

Right now, we need to focus on certain items on the form. Three pages from the Uniform Application are shown here with notes on each of the numbered items.

1. **LOAN AMOUNT:** If there is any doubt, leave this section blank. Talk with your loan agent about -the workability and adequacy of the amount you have in mind. The amount is likely to change over the course of the transaction anyway, and your initial estimate will be acceptable.

2. **INTEREST RATE:** Leave blank. There may be several changes, and your agent will insert the right figure at the right time.

3. **PROPERTY ADDRESS**: This is the property that is being financed and that will be used as security. Double-check the numbers and spellings.

4. **LEGAL DESCRIPTION**: Leave the space blank. Your agent will complete it for you.

5. **YEAR ACQUIRED/ORIGINAL COST**: This section is needed only for refinancing or construction take out.

6. **PURPOSE OF REFINANCE:** State whether your purpose is for improved rate and pay ment, debt consolidation, home improvement, or something else.

7. **LEGAL TITLE VESTING:** This is the place to designate the manner in which the title will be held (joint tenancy, undivided half interest, etc.) If you're not certain on this one, get professional consultation.

39

8. **EMPLOYMENT:** Here, you'll need to supply those last two years federal tax returns and W-2s and a current pay stub. The self-employed need those tax returns, that year-to-date profit and loss statement, and a current balance sheet.

9. **PRIOR EMPLOYMENT:** Having solid employment goes a long way on loan approval. Don't skip this one if you have been on your present job less than two years. Provide information as requested on the application and make sure there are no gaps in your employment.

10. **MONTHLY INCOME:** In this section, do write your estimated gross monthly income. You will, of course, need all possible documentation of income.

#18 | **HELPFUL HINT:** At any point that you do not have room to get all your information in the space provided, write: "See Attachment" and prepare a neat, clear statement or chart-appropriately titled and preferably typed. If you have more than one attachment, supply numbers or names or both so that there will be no delays or confusion.

40

11. PRESENT AND PROPOSED PAYMENTS: Include your present monthly rent or mortgage obligations. If you are currently obligated to pay a home owner's association fee, it will be necessary for your agent to contact the association for specific information. Please include telephone number and address. Leave the proposed payment section blank.

12. BANKING AND CREDIT RELATIONSHIPS: This is a likely place for one of those attachments. Have all those items listed earlier under other assets (stocks, bonds, personal property) and checking and savings accounts (names, addresses, account numbers, balances) ready.

13. REAL ESTATE YOU OWN: First, complete the Schedule of Real Estate Owned, Section 15. Show all real estate you now own, including any which is income producing. Then enter the total in Section 13. Include the home you presently own even if it's sold and you have not yet received the proceeds.

14. LIABILITIES/REAL ESTATE LOANS: Here is another place that you might provide an attachment to give all the information called for under Credit History above: all installment debts, credit cards with a balance, auto loans, student loans, personal loans-everything. Do the same for real estate loans. Double check names, addresses, account numbers, and balances due.

Uniform Residential Loan Application

This application is designed to be completed by the Borrower(s) with the Lender's assistance. The Co-Borrower Section and all other Co-Borrower questions must be completed and the appropriate box(es) checked if [X] another person will be jointly obligated with the Borrower on the loan, or ☐ the Borrower is relying on income from alimony, child support or separate maintenance or on the income or assets of another person as a basis for repayment of the loan, or ☐ the Borrower is married and resides in, or the property is located in, a community property state.

I. TYPE OF MORTGAGE AND TERMS OF LOAN

Mortgage Applied for:	☐ VA [X] Conventional ☐ Other: ☐ FHA ☐ FmHA	Agency Case Number	Lender Case No.

Amount	Ir Rate	No. of Months	Amortization Type:		
$ 96,600 **1**	**2** 10.0 %	360	[X] Fixed Rate ☐ GPM	☐ Other (explain): ☐ ARM (type):	

II. PROPERTY INFORMATION AND PURPOSE OF LOAN

Subject Property Address (street, city, state, & zip code)	No. of Units
511 American Dream Street, Ameriville, WZ 26000 **3**	1

Legal Description of Subject Property (attach description if necessary)	Year Built
See Attached **4**	1982

Purpose of Loan	[X] Purchase ☐ Construction ☐ Other (explain): ☐ Refinance ☐ Construction-Permanent	Property will be: [X] Primary Residence ☐ Secondary Residence ☐ Investment

Complete this line if construction or construction-permanent loan.

Year Lot Acquired	Original Cost	Amount Existing Liens	(a) Present Value of Lot	(b) Cost of Improvements	Total (a + b)
5	$	$	$	$	$

Complete this line if this is a refinance loan.

Year Acquired	Original Cost	Amount Existing Liens	Purpose of Refinance	Describe Improvements ☐ made ☐ to be made
	$	$	**6**	Cost: $

Title will be held in what Name(s)	Manner in which Title will be held	Estate will be held in:
Shirley and Duke Smith **7**	Joint Tenancy	[X] Fee Simple ☐ Leasehold (show expiration date)

Source of Down Payment, Settlement Charges and/or Subordinate Financing (explain)
Savings

III. BORROWER INFORMATION

	Borrower	Co-Borrower
Name (include Jr. or Sr. if applicable)	Duke Smith	Shirley Smith

	Social Security Number	Home Phone (incl. area code)	Age	Yrs. School	Social Security Number	Home Phone (incl. area code)	Age	Yrs. School
	001-23-4567	(000) 555-1111	27	14	002-23-4567	(000) 555-1111	25	15

Borrower	Co-Borrower
[X] Married ☐ Unmarried (include single, divorced, widowed) ☐ Separated Dependents (not listed by Co-Borrower) no. 1 ages 18 months	[X] Married ☐ Unmarried (include single, divorced, widowed) ☐ Separated Dependents (not listed by Borrower) no. 1 ages 18 months
Present Address (street, city, state, zip code) ☐ Own [X] Rent 5 No. Yrs.	Present Address (street, city, state, zip code) ☐ Own [X] Rent 5 No. Yrs.
1902 Glen Drive Ameriville, WZ 26000	Same

If residing at present address for less than seven years, complete the following:

Former Address (street, city, state, zip code) ☐ Own [X] Rent 3 No. Yrs.	Former Address (street, city, state, zip code) ☐ Own [X] Rent 2 No. Yrs.
6238 Sampson Street Ameriville, WZ 26000	6314 Albatross Drive Ameriville, WZ 26000

Former Address (street, city, state, zip code) ☐ Own ☐ Rent ___ No. Yrs.	Former Address (street, city, state, zip code) ☐ Own ☐ Rent ___ No. Yrs.

IV. EMPLOYMENT INFORMATION

	Borrower	Co-Borrower

Name & Address of Employer ☐ Self Employed	Yrs. on this job	Name & Address of Employer ☐ Self Employed	Yrs. on this job
Car Land 234 Oak Street Ameriville, WZ 26000 **8**	6 Yrs. employed in this line of work/profession 3	City School System Junior High School Ameriville, WZ 26000	3 Yrs. employed in this line of work/profession 3

Position/Title/Type of Business	Business Phone (incl. area code)	Position/Title/Type of Business	Business Phone (incl. area code)
Auto Mechanic/Auto Dealership	(000) 555-2222	Teacher Aide/Education	(000) 555-3333

If employed in current position for less than two years or if currently employed in more than one position, complete the following:

Name & Address of Employer ☐ Self Employed	Dates (from - to)	Name & Address of Employer ☐ Self Employed	Dates (from - to)
9	Monthly Income $		Monthly Income $

Position/Title/Type of Business	Business Phone (incl. area code)	Position/Title/Type of Business	Business Phone (incl. area code)

Name & Address of Employer ☐ Self Employed	Dates (from - to)	Name & Address of Employer ☐ Self Employed	Dates (from - to)
	Monthly Income $		Monthly Income $

Position/Title/Type of Business	Business Phone (incl. area code)	Position/Title/Type of Business	Business Phone (incl. area code)

41

15. SCHEDULE OF REAL ESTATE OWNED: Complete this section or provide an attachment to show all your properties.

16. PURCHASE PRICE: Leave this section blank if this is a refinance. If it is a purchase, enter the purchase price and include a copy of the purchase agreement. Leave the rest of the section blank.

17. DECLARATIONS: Please answer "yes" or "no" to each question. If you answer it yes" to any question, attach a letter of explanation. If you answer, "yes" to bankruptcy, attach a copy of the Discharge of Bankruptcy. If you are divorced, attach a stamped copy of your final Divorce Settlement and Interlocutory Decree.

18. CITIZENSHIP INFORMATION/OCCUPANCY OF SUBJECT PROPERTY: Provide information as called for. Your application cannot be processed unless you check the boxes in this section. It is a federal offense to misrepresent your intentions.

19. SIGNATURES: Please read carefully the section titled "Acknowledgment and Agreement." Then, each applicant must sign and date in ink.

20. MONITORING INFORMATION: The federal government wants to monitor lenders to preclude discrimination in lending on the basis of race, national origin, or sex but, at the same time,does not want to invade privacy by requiring the borrower to give that information. If the borrower doesn't provide the information, the lender (loan agent) must mark the boxes. To avoid errors, your loan agent requests that you provide the information.

That, in summary, is what you can expect as far as actually making the application is concerned. More will happen at that meeting. Your loan officer will answer your questions, explain what happens the rest of the way, and explain various forms. You'll want to ask what you can do to make yourself look your very best to the lender.

V. MONTHLY INCOME AND COMBINED HOUSING EXPENSE INFORMATION

Gross Monthly Income	Borrower	Co-Borrower	Total	Combined Monthly Housing Expense	Present	Proposed
Base Empl. Income *	$ 1,700	$ 1,083	2,783	Rent	$ 725	▓▓▓▓▓▓
Overtime	300		300	First Mortgage (P&I)		$ 848
Bonuses				Other Financing (P&I)		
Commissions				Hazard Insurance		26
Dividends/Interest	**10**			Real Estate Taxes	**11**	97
Net Rental Income				Mortgage Insurance		48
Other (before completing, see the notice in "describe other income," below)				Homeowner Assn. Dues		
				Other:		
Total	$ 2,000	$ 1,083	$ 3,083	Total	$ 725	$ 1,019

* Self Employed Borrower(s) may be required to provide additional documentation such as tax returns and financial statements.

Describe Other Income *Notice:* Alimony, child support, or separate maintenance income need not be revealed if the Borrower (B) or Co-Borrower (C) does not choose to have it considered for repaying this loan.

B/C		Monthly Amount
		$

VI. ASSETS AND LIABILITIES

This Statement and any applicable supporting schedules may be completed jointly by both married and unmarried Co-Borrowers if their assets and liabilities are sufficiently joined so that the Statement can be meaningfully and fairly presented on a combined basis; otherwise separate Statements and Schedules are required. If the Co-Borrower section was completed about a spouse, this Statement and supporting schedules must be completed about that spouse also.

Completed ☐ Jointly ☐ Not Jointly

ASSETS Description	Cash or Market Value	Liabilities and Pledged Assets. List the creditor's name, address and account number for all outstanding debts, including automobile loans, revolving charge accounts, real estate loans, alimony, child support, stock pledges, etc. Use continuation sheet, if necessary. Indicate by (*) those liabilities which will be satisfied upon sale of real estate owned or upon refinancing of the subject property.	Monthly Payt. & Mos. Left to Pay	Unpaid Balance
Cash deposit toward purchase held by:		LIABILITIES Name and address of Company	$ Payt./Mos.	$
ABC Realty	2,000	Ameriville Dept. Store **14**		
		301 Main Street	10/16	160
List checking and savings accounts below		Ameriville, WZ 26000		
Name and address of Bank, S&L, or Credit Union				
Dollar Bank **12**		Acct. no. 23-45-678		
101 Main Street		Name and address of Company	$ Payt./Mos.	$
Ameriville, WZ 26000		Dollar Bank		
		101 Main Street	110/2	220
Acct. no. 12345678	$SA 3,125	Ameriville, WZ, 26000		
Name and address of Bank, S&L, or Credit Union				
Good Cents Bank		Acct. no. 34-56-789		
200 Main Street		Name and address of Company	$ Payt./Mos.	$
Ameriville, WZ 26000		Master Card		
	SA 1,000	123 White Street	29/18	522
Acct. no. 2345678	$CK 965	Ameriville, WZ 26000		
Name and address of Bank, S&L, or Credit Union				
		Acct. no. 2030405060		
		Name and address of Company	$ Payt./Mos.	$
Acct. no.	$			
Name and address of Bank, S&L, or Credit Union		Acct. no.		
		Name and address of Company	$ Payt./Mos.	$
Acct. no.	$			
Stocks & Bonds (Company name/number & description)	$			
		Acct. no.		
		Name and address of Company	$ Payt./Mos.	$
Life insurance net cash value	$			
Face amount: $				
Subtotal Liquid Assets	$			
Real estate owned (enter market value from schedule of real estate owned)	$ **13**	Acct. no.		
Vested interest in retirement fund	$	Name and address of Company	$ Payt./Mos.	$
Net worth of business(es) owned (attach financial statement)	$			
Automobiles owned (make and year)	$			
1987 Dodge	5,000			
		Acct. no.		
		Alimony/Child Support/Separate Maintenance Payments Owed to:	$	▓▓▓▓▓
Other Assets (itemize)	$	Job Related Expense (child care, union dues, etc.)	$	▓▓▓▓▓
Furniture and Personal Property	10,000			
		Total Monthly Payments	$ 149	
Total Assets a.	$ 22,090	Net Worth (a minus b) $	Total Liabilities b.	$ 902

43

VI. ASSETS AND LIABILITIES (cont.)

Schedule of Real Estate Owned (If additional properties are owned, use continuation sheet.)

Property Address (enter S if sold, PS if pending sale or R if rental being held for income)	Type of Property	Present Market Value	Amount of Mortgages & Liens	Gross Rental Income	Mortgage Payments	Insurance, Maintenance, Taxes & Misc.	Net Rental Income
15		$	$	$	$	$	$
Totals		$	$	$	$	$	$

List any additional names under which credit has previously been received and indicate appropriate creditor name(s) and account number(s):

Alternate Name	Creditor Name	Account Number

VII. DETAILS OF TRANSACTION

a. Purchase price **16**	$ 101,750
b. Alterations, improvements, repairs	
c. Land (if acquired separately)	
d. Refinance (incl. debts to be paid off)	
e. Estimated prepaid items	814
f. Estimated closing costs	5,088
g. PMI, MIP, Funding Fee paid in cash	
h. Discount (if Borrower will pay)	
i. Total costs (add items a through h)	107,652
j. Subordinate financing	
k. Borrower's closing costs paid by Seller	3,000
l. Other Credits (explain) Cash Deposit	2,000
m. Loan amount (exclude PMI, MIP, Funding Fee financed)	96,600
n. PMI, MIP, Funding Fee financed	
o. Loan amount (add m & n)	96,600
p. Cash from/to Borrower (subtract j, k, l & o from i)	6,052

VIII. DECLARATIONS

If you answer "yes" to any questions a through i, please use continuation sheet for explanation. **17**

	Borrower Yes	Borrower No	Co-Borrower Yes	Co-Borrower No
a. Are there any outstanding judgments against you?		X		X
b. Have you been declared bankrupt within the past 7 years?		X		X
c. Have you had property foreclosed upon or given title or deed in lieu thereof in the last 7 years?		X		X
d. Are you a party to a lawsuit?		X		X
e. Have you directly or indirectly been obligated on any loan which resulted in foreclosure, transfer of title in lieu of foreclosure, or judgment? (This would include such loans as home mortgage loans, SBA loans, home improvement loans, educational loans, manufactured (mobile) home loans, any mortgage, financial obligation, bond, or loan guarantee. If "Yes," provide details, including date, name and address of Lender, FHA or VA case number, if any, and reasons for the action.)		X		X
f. Are you presently delinquent or in default on any Federal debt or any other loan, mortgage, financial obligation, bond, or loan guarantee? If "Yes," give details as described in the preceding question.		X		X
g. Are you obligated to pay alimony, child support, or separate maintenance?		X		X
h. Is any part of the down payment borrowed?		X		X
i. Are you a co-maker or endorser on a note?		X		X
j. Are you a U.S. citizen? **18**	X		X	
k. Are you a permanent resident alien?		X		X
l. Do you intend to occupy the property as your primary residence?	X		X	

IX. ACKNOWLEDGMENT AND AGREEMENT

The undersigned specifically acknowledge(s) and agree(s) that: (1) the loan requested by this application will be secured by a first mortgage or deed of trust on the property described herein; (2) the property will not be used for any illegal or prohibited purpose or use; (3) all statements made in this application are made for the purpose of obtaining the loan indicated herein; (4) occupation of the property will be as indicated above; (5) verification or reverification of any information contained in the application may be made at any time by the Lender, its agents, successors and assigns, either directly or through a credit reporting agency, from any source named in this application, and the original copy of this application will be retained by the Lender, even if the loan is not approved; (6) the Lender, its agents, successors and assigns will rely on the information contained in the application and I/we have a continuing obligation to amend and/or supplement the information provided in this application if any of the material facts which I/we have represented herein should change prior to closing; (7) in the event my/our payments on the loan indicated in this application become delinquent, the Lender, its agents, successors and assigns, may, in addition to all their other rights and remedies, report my/our name(s) and account information to a credit reporting agency; (8) ownership of the loan may be transferred to successor or assign of the Lender without notice to me and/or the administration of the loan account may be transferred to an agent, successor or assign of the Lender with prior notice to me; (9) the Lender, its agents, successors and assigns make no representations or warranties, express or implied, to the Borrower(s) regarding the property, the condition of the property, or the value of the property.

Certification: I/We certify that the information provided in this application is true and correct as of the date set forth opposite my/our signature(s) on this application and acknowledge my/our understanding that any intentional or negligent misrepresentation(s) of the information contained in this application may result in civil liability and/or criminal penalties including, but not limited to, fine or imprisonment or both under the provisions of Title 18, United States Code, Section 1001, et seq. and liability for monetary damages to the Lender, its agents, successors and assigns, insurers and any other person who may suffer any loss due to reliance upon any misrepresentation which I/we have made on this application.

Borrower's Signature **19**	Date	Co-Borrower's Signature	Date
X _(signature)_	1/15/92	X _Shirley Smith_	1/15/92

X. INFORMATION FOR GOVERNMENT MONITORING PURPOSES

The following information is requested by the Federal Government for certain types of loans related to a dwelling, in order to monitor the Lender's compliance with equal credit opportunity, fair housing and home mortgage disclosure laws. You are not required to furnish this information, but are encouraged to do so. The law provides that a Lender may neither discriminate on the basis of this information, nor on whether you choose to furnish it. However, if you choose not to furnish it, under Federal regulations this Lender is required to note race and sex on the basis of visual observation or surname. If you do not wish to furnish the above information, please check the box below. (Lender must review the above material to assure that the disclosures satisfy all requirements to which the Lender is subject under applicable state law for the particular type of loan applied for.)

BORROWER **20**

☐ I do not wish to furnish this information

Race/National Origin:
☐ American Indian or Alaskan Native ☐ Asian or Pacific Islander
☐ Black, not of Hispanic origin ☐ Hispanic ☐ White, not of Hispanic origin

Sex: ☐ Female ☐ Male

CO-BORROWER

☐ I do not wish to furnish this information

Race/National Origin:
☐ American Indian or Alaskan Native ☐ Asian or Pacific Islander
☐ Black, not of Hispanic origin ☐ Hispanic ☐ White, not of Hispanic origin

Sex: ☐ Female ☐ Male

To be Completed by Interviewer		
This application was taken by:	Interviewer's Name (print or type) U. R. Banker	Name and Address of Interviewer's Employer
☒ face-to-face interview	Interviewer's Signature _(signature)_ Date	Ameriville Bank & Trust
☐ by mail		100 Main Street
☐ by telephone	Interviewer's Phone Number (incl. area code) (000) 555-5555	Ameriville, WZ 26000

Freddie Mac Form 65/Rev. 5/91 (Amended)

Fannie Mae Form 1003/Rev. 5/91 (Amended)

44

Locking Your Rate

One of the other things that will probably be discussed during the taking of your application is the question of whether to let the loan rate float or to lock the rate. (You could lock the day of the application.) In a downward market, there is little or no advantage in locking, so very little need be said; in an upward market, such as occurred in the mid to late 1980s, locking could be advantageous and calls for attention. What you do is determined in part by your reading of the current market, by your loan agent's advice, and by your gambling instinct. If you let the rate float throughout the processing of the loan, you'll have available the interest rate in effect when your loan is approved-or after your loan is approved if you do not close immediately. If you say that you want a 30 day lock at one particular day's interest rate, then for 30 days your interest rate can go no higher. If your loan doesn't close in 30 days, then your rate may be increased to new market rates, and/or you may be subject to a penalty.

Please note that having a locked rate does not constitute loan approval.

There are several things to consider before making a decision.

➤   There is usually a cost for locking rates over a longer period (60 days). Lenders want to protect themselves in the event that rates go up while they are committed to lower rates. Locks for extended periods, therefore, carry higher interest rates or points.

➤   The rise and fall of interest rates may go counter to the predictions of the best experts. If interest rates are definitely rising and the prospect is that they will continue to do so, obviously you should lock. Conversely, with falling rates, you should not. When, however, the market is volatile and experts are divided in their predictions of which direction rates will go, you have a difficult decision with at least as much chance of being wrong as being right.

➤   Most of the advertised rates that you receive in the mail are based on short-term locks. You will not be entitled to those rates until your loan is approved, and that may be 30 days or more from that date. Do not be swayed by posted rates; they will probably change by the time you are ready to lock.

➤ The length of time for locking the loan has to be coordinated with the likely time of closing. Some documents, including the loan approval, may have expiration dates. Once your loan is locked for a set number of days, you have that many days for the loan to be funded; if it isn't, you may be subject to penalties and may have to go back through the approval process. Short-term locks (10-15 days) are not offered unless the loan has already been approved. Long-term locks (45-60 days) allow more time for something (a new credit problem, a question about income, a drop in property values, buyer's remorse) to block approval of the loan. Lenders are likely to offer their best rates if they know that in two weeks they'll have funds from a loan but not likely to offer good rates when there will be a month or two's delay and possible problems. You may, therefore, choose to wait until the loan is approved and take the best rate you can get without actually locking the rate.

➤ When you make a 7 to 10 day lock (short term), you are at the mercy of the closing agent's schedule. It takes 2 days to prepare legal documents and get them to the closing agent. Add 3 days for rescission on a refinance, 1 day to fund, and 1 day to record. There are 7 days gone. When you get the call to sign loan documents, you must be ready to go. Failure to stay within the time limits could be costly-but that's the way you get the lowest price.

➤ Your loan agent may or may not be helpful. The interests of the agent may not be the same as yours. The agent may inspire less and less confidence as the process continues - a reason for choosing your agent with care. The agent should, however, give you an accurate picture of your options.

46

#19 HELPFUL HINT: When you shop for interest rates, ask the cost of locking a rate. Ask who gets a fee. Keep in mind that loan agents receive incentives for offering loans at rates higher than market rates and for shorter locking terms.

There is no point in your getting anxious about when or whether to lock. Get what information you can; weigh what you get. Watch the progress of you loan and movement of rates. Then, when and if the time comes, make the best decision you can and be pleased with the way you made it.

#20 Before you start gathering materials, study Chapter Four on the processing of a loan, especially the opening section and the section on the reading of a credit report. The information in the two chapters fits into a single picture for seeing ways to get ready and ways to go.

You've had enough detail for the moment. Take a break and then get back on course for getting through the mortgage maze.

Chapter Four

On the Road through the Maze:

Processing the Loan

Behind the loan agent is a loan processor, the person who assembles your file, the one who orders your credit report, verifies your employment and income, orders the appraisal (or gets it into the file if the loan agent orders it), gets the title report, orders escrow or closing instructions, and, in short, makes certain that every form, every report required is in your file.

The loan agent and the loan processor work together to coordinate all documentation. In a limited operation, one person may do everything. In a sophisticated operation, there is a full office staff. In addition to the loan processor, there is, for example, a loan opener or data entry person who puts the entire loan application into the computer, making it possible to correct or add information and produce a completely new application in minutes.

You may or may not meet the loan processor. You may or may not speak with the loan processor. The loan processor stays at the desk, pulling together a dozen, two dozen, three dozen files. Part of the time your file will be on the top, part of the time on the bottom. If that missing document has just arrived or if it is noted that the document has not arrived, your file is in the processor's hands. If documents are arriving in good time, your file is in its place and waiting. (If you telephone when your file is in the processor's hands, you get an immediate response; if you call at another time, it may take a few minutes.)

The most efficient loan processors utilize computers to keep files up to date and to show the status of all files in a few seconds. With the right kind of computer program, the processor can, at the beginning of the day, at the end of the day, or at any time during the day, see everything that is needed for every file in progress in a matter of minutes. There is no need to go through forty sheets of paper, trying to decipher notes and check marks. And the processor has a much clearer, much more graphic picture of the status of all work in progress.

When the loan processor sees that a document has not arrived, the processor contacts whoever was to provide that document: a credit card company, an employer, or you. The faster those documents are made available-fax, messenger, personal delivery-the faster your loan will be processed. If your loan processor calls and asks for something that shows that you receive a monthly check for $103.84 from a family trust fund, ask how long you have to get it there; then get it there.

Unless all your income is from one or two regular sources and all your debts are to a few well-known creditors, you can expect to be asked for added documentation. If you get residuals from your days as a child actor, receive curious little quarterly checks from an option on an oil lease, moonlight from time to time as a paperhanger, have a stack of accounts receivable from shaky companies, or collect $50 a month on a loan to your son-in-law, expect to be asked for extra documentation. Ask your loan agent the best and strongest ways to verify such income.

Don't try to persuade the loan processor (or the loan agent) that you really do have that income; the task is for both (or all) of you, together, to persuade the person who makes the decision. Spend the time and effort required to get the best documentation possible to the loan processor as soon as possible.

Be prepared that lenders may not consider some income. If you're depending on every cent to qualify for the loan, you could have a problem. Make sure that your loan agent understands. Discuss all details to avoid surprises for your loan agent and for you.

You can expect to be asked for information that you are certain you have already provided. Be annoyed or get angry as you will, but get the information in as quickly as possible. Incidentally, such possibilities are good reason for getting all your materials together and keeping them together rather than putting them away.

Expect your loan processor to do a super job, but note that loan processors generally do not make loan decisions or discuss interest rates. Save your questions and requests for your loan agent.

Typically the work of the loan processor takes fifteen to twenty days. Getting loan approval, funding the loan, and getting through escrow will add enough time in the mortgage maze that you do not want any delays in processing. While many matters may be out of your control, you can make certain that you respond to calls for information or documentation promptly, and often you can-with some initiative-make things move faster. You might get quicker responses from your employer or companies with whom you do business. You might have or find access to information that would clear a road block in completing the appraisal.

#21 | **HELPFUL HINT:** Be available. Be prepared. Be involved in the process. The way that you approach the process can make a difference in the results.

49

<u>Getting Forms on File</u>

You will be introduced to several forms during your loan application or soon after. Some of the forms you will keep; some you will complete and return; some will go to other parties who have interest or involvement in the loan. All of them have to on file somewhere. The necessity for all the forms may not be apparent, but the people who run the lending business rely on them for a variety of reasons. Remember that lenders are particularly sensitive to the thought of bad loans and that regulations require compliance. Groan if you will at the paperwork, but do read everything and take any action called for; it is the system.

The main forms are shown and identified on the

next few pages.

The descriptions given are all that most borrowers in most situations need to know about the forms, but in any individual case, there may be a need for more information; if you have questions about any of the forms, do ask.

> NOTE: Particular lenders may require other documentation specific to their needs; there may be additional forms not discussed here.

Good Faith Estimate (GFE)

Lenders and brokers are required by the Real Estate Settlement Procedures Act to give a borrower a list of estimated fees and charges that the borrower will have to pay-or have added to the loan. To protect themselves, lenders stress that it is an estimate and subject to change. The Good Faith Estimate is not always treated seriously; loan agents have in effect said, "Oh, don't pay any attention to that. It's just something we have to do." It is to be hoped that most agents do put good faith-and some serious thought-into the GFE. You are certainly justified in asking what might change, how much, and why. (You'll find a list of fees at the end of this chapter.)

Lender:

Address:

Applicant(s):

Property:

GOOD FAITH ESTIMATE

Sales Price:

Base Loan Amount:

Total Loan Amount:

Type of Loan:

Date:

The information provided below reflects estimates of the charges which you are likely to incur at the settlement of your loan. The fees listed are estimates - the actual charges may be more or less. Your transaction may not involve a fee for every item listed.

The numbers listed beside the estimates generally correspond to the numbered lines contained in the HUD-1 settlement statement which you will be receiving at settlement. The HUD-1 settlement statement will show you the actual cost for items paid at settlement.

800   ITEMS PAYABLE IN CONNECTION WITH LOAN

801	Loan Origination Fee	%	$
802	Loan Discount	%	$
803	Appraisal Fee		$
804	Credit Report		$
805	Lender's Inspection Fee		$
806	Mortgage Insurance Application Fee		$
807	Assumption Fee		$
808	Mortgage Broker Fee		$
809	CLO Access Fee		$
810	Tax Related Service Fee		$
			$
			$
			$

900   ITEMS REQUIRED BY LENDER TO BE PAID IN ADVANCE

901	Interest for	days @ $	per day	$
902	Mortgage Insurance Premium			$
903	Hazard Insurance Premium			$
904				$

1000   RESERVES DEPOSITED WITH LENDER

1001	Hazard Insurance Premiums	months @ $	per month	$
	Tax and Assessment Reserves	months @ $	per month	$
				$

1100   TITLE CHARGES

1101	Closing or Escrow Fee	$
1102	Abstract or Title Search	$
1103	Title Examination	$
1105	Document Preparation Fee	$
1107	Attorney Fees	$
1108	Title Insurance	$
		$

1200   GOVERNMENT RECORDING & TRANSFER CHARGES

1201	Recording Fees: Deed: $	; Mortgage: $	; Release $	$
1202	City/County Tax/Stamps: Deed: $	; Mortgage: $	; Release: $	$
1203	State Tax/Stamps: Deed: $	; Mortgage: $		$

1300   ADDITIONAL SETTLEMENT CHARGES

1301	Survey	$
1302	Pest Inspection	$
		$
		$

TOTAL ESTIMATED SETTLEMENT CHARGES $

"S" designates those costs to be paid by Seller.

TOTAL ESTIMATED FUNDS NEEDED TO CLOSE

Downpayment	$
Est. Closing Costs	$
Est. Prepaid Items/Reserves	$
OTHER:	$
TOTAL EST. FUNDS NEEDED TO CLOSE	$

TOTAL ESTIMATED MONTHLY PAYMENT

Principal & Interest	$
Real Estate Taxes	$
Flood & Hazard Insurance	$
Mortgage Insurance	$
TOTAL MONTHLY PAYMENT	$

THIS SECTION TO BE COMPLETED BY LENDER ONLY IF A PARTICULAR PROVIDER OF SERVICE IS REQUIRED. Use of the particular provider is required and the estimate is based on charges of the provider.

ITEM NO.	NAME & ADDRESS OF PROVIDER	TELEPHONE NO.	NATURE OF RELATIONSHIP

These estimates are provided pursuant to the Real Estate Settlement Procedures Act of 1974, as amended (RESPA). Additional information can be found in the HUD Special Information Booklet, which is to be provided to you by your mortgage broker or lender. The undersigned acknowledges receipt of the booklet "Settlement Costs," and if applicable the Consumer Handbook on ARM Mortgages.

Applicant	Date	Applicant	Date
Applicant	Date	Applicant	Date

FE-770R

VMP-770R (9212)

12/92

VMP MORTGAGE FORMS • (800)521-7291

Borrowers' Consent Form

The loan processor can't get certain information about you without your approval. The borrower's consent form allows the loan processor to get that information without your having to sign many separate requests. The form is an affidavit of your signature.

BORROWER CONSENT

I/We hereby give our consent to Quest Financial Group, Inc., or any reporting bureau which it may designate, to obtain any and all information concerning our savings and/or checking accounts, our employment, our credit obligations and all other credit matters which they may require in connection with our application for a loan. This form may be reproduced or photocopied and copy shall be as effective as the original which I/We have signed.

_____   _____
Borrower   Date

_____   _____
Borrower   Date

_____   _____
Borrower   Date

I hereby certify this to be a true and correct copy of the original.

_____   _____
Quest Financial Group, Inc.   Date

53

Request for Verification of Rent or Mortgage Account (VOM)

The lender to whom you are applying wants to know how regularly and promptly you have paid others, so this form goes to your current mortgage lender or landlord to verify payment history. Some lenders report your mortgage information on a credit report. Therefore, this form may not be needed.

Request for Verification of Rent or Mortgage Account

Privacy Act Notice: This information is to be used by the agency collecting it or its assignees in determining whether you qualify as a prospective mortgagor under its program. It will not be disclosed outside the agency except as required and permitted by law. You do not have to provide this information, but if you do not your application for approval as a prospective mortgagor or borrower may be delayed or rejected. The information requested in this form is authorized by Title 38, USC, Chapter 37 (if V.A.); by 12 USC, Section 1701 et. seq. (if HUD/FHA); by 42 USC, Section 1452b (if HUD/CPD); and Title 42 USC, 1471 et. seq., or 7 USC, 1921 et. seq. (if USDA/FmHA).

Instructions: Lender - Complete items 1 through 8. Have applicant(s) complete item 9. Lender then will forward directly to creditor named in item 1.
Landlord/Creditor - Please complete items 10 through 18 and return directly to lender named in item 2.
The form is to be transmitted directly to the lender and is not to be transmitted through the applicant(s) or any other party.

Part I - Request

1. To (Name and address of landlord/creditor)	2. From (Name and address of lender)

I certify that this verification has been sent directly to the landlord/creditor and has not passed through the hands of the applicant or any other party.

3. Signature of Lender	4. Title	5. Date	6. Lender's Number (Optional)

7. Information To Be Verified

Property Address	Account in the Name of	Account Number
	☐ Mortgage ☐ Rental ☐ Land Contract ☐	

I have applied for a mortgage loan. My signature below authorizes verification of mortgage or rent information.

8. Name and Address of Applicant(s)	9. Signature of Applicant(s)
	X X

Part II - To Be Completed by Landlord/Creditor

We have received an application for a loan from the above, to whom we understand you rent or have extended a loan. In addition to the information requested below please furnish us with any information you might have that will assist us in processing of the loan.

☐ Rental Account ☐ Mortgage Account or ☐ Land Contract

10. Tenant rented from_____
to_____
Amount of rent $_____per_____
Number of late payments_____*
Is account satisfactory? ☐ Yes ☐ No
_____
_____
_____

11. Date account opened_____
Original contract amount $_____
Current account balance $_____
Monthly payment P & I only $_____
Payment with taxes & ins. $_____
Is account current? ☐ Yes ☐ No
Was loan assumed? ☐ Yes ☐ No
Satisfactory account? ☐ Yes ☐ No

12. Interest rate_____%
☐ FIXED ☐ ARM
☐ FHA ☐ V.A.
☐ CONV. ☐ OTHER_____
Next pay date_____
No. of late payments_____*
No. of late charges_____
Owner of First Mortgage
☐ FNMA ☐ FHLMC ☐ Seller/Other

*Payment History for the previous 12 months must be provided in order to comply with secondary mortgage market requirements.

13. Additional information which may be of assistance in determination of credit worthiness

Part III — Authorized Signature

Federal statutes provide severe penalties for any fraud, intentional misrepresentation, or criminal connivance or conspiracy purposed to influence the issuance of any guaranty or insurance by the V.A. Secretary, the USDA, FmHA/FHA Commissioner, or the HUD/CPD Assistant Secretary.

14. Signature of Landlord/Creditor Representative	15. Title (Please print or type)	16. Date

17. Print or type name signed in item 14

18. Phone No.

3/93

FE-43

VMP -43 (9303) VMP MORTGAGE FORMS • (800)521-7291

LANDLORD/CREDITOR-RETURN BOTH COPIES TO LENDER

55

<u>Request for Verification of Deposit (VOD)</u>

Like the VOM, the VOD is a way of establishing your qualification for a loan. The VOD is sent to banking institutions for current information about your accounts. Sometimes your bank will not provide an average balance on an account; when that happens, it is likely that your processor or agent will ask for bank statements for the last three months.

Request for Verification of Deposit

FannieMae

Privacy Act Notice: This information is to be used by the agency collecting it or its assignees in determining whether you qualify as a prospective mortgagor under its program. It will not be disclosed outside the agency except as required and permitted by law. You do not have to provide this information, but if you do not your application for approval as a prospective mortgagor or borrower may be delayed or rejected. The information requested in this form is authorized by Title 38, USC, Chapter 37 (if VA); by 12 USC, Section 1701 et. seq. (if HUD/FHA); by 42 USC, Section 1452b (if HUD/CPD); and Title 42 USC, 1471 et. seq., or 7 USC, 1921 et. seq. (if USDA/FmHA).

Instructions: Lender - Complete items 1 through 8. Have applicant(s) complete item 9. Forward directly to depository named in item 1.
Depository - Please complete items 10 through 18 and return directly to lender named in item 2.
The form is to be transmitted directly to the lender and is not to be transmitted through the applicant(s) or any other party.

Part I - Request

1. To (Name and address of depository)	2. From (Name and address of lender)

I certify that this verification has been sent directly to the bank or depository and has not passed through the hands of the applicant or any other party.

3. Signature of Lender	4. Title	5. Date	6. Lender's No. (Optional)

7. Information To Be Verified

Type of Account	Account in Name of	Account Number	Balance
			$
			$
			$
			$

To Depository: I/We have applied for a mortgage loan and stated in my financial statement that the balance on deposit with you is as shown above. You are authorized to verify this information and to supply the lender identified above with the information requested in items 10 through 13. Your response is solely a matter of courtesy for which no responsibility is attached to your institution or any of your officers.

8. Name and Address of Applicant(s)	9. Signature of Applicant(s)
	X
	X

To Be Completed by Depository

Part II - Verification of Depository

10. Deposit Accounts of Applicant(s)

Type of Account	Account Number	Current Balance	Average Balance For Previous Two Months	Date Opened
		$	$	
		$	$	
		$	$	
		$	$	

11. Loans Outstanding To Applicant(s)

Loan Number	Date of Loan	Original Amount	Current Balance	Installments (Monthly/Quarterly)	Secured By	No. of Late Pymts.
		$	$	$ per		
		$	$	$ per		
		$	$	$ per		

12. Please include any additional information which may be of assistance in determination of credit worthiness. (Please include information on loans paid-in-full in item 11 above.)

13. If the name(s) on the account(s) differ from those listed in item 7, please supply the name(s) on the account(s) as reflected by your records.

Part III — Authorized Signature - Federal statutes provide severe penalties for any fraud, intentional misrepresentation, or criminal connivance or conspiracy purposed to influence the issuance of any guaranty or insurance by the VA Secretary, the USDA, FmHA/FHA Commissioner, or the HUD/CPD Assistant Secretary.

14. Signature of Depository Representative	15. Title (Please print or type)	16. Date

17. Please print or type name signed in item 14

18. Phone No.

Fannie Mae
Form 1006 Mar. 90

VMP -41 (9007).02   VMP MORTGAGE FORMS • (800)521-7291

FE-41

DEPOSITORY-RETURN BOTH COPIES TO LENDER

57

Request for Verification of Gift/Gift Letter

If you have a benefactor who makes you an outright gift of a down payment for a purchase or a pay down for a refinance, this form explains your source of funds to let the lender know that you did not borrow that money. It acts as a VOD.

58

Request for Verification of Gift/Gift Letter

Privacy Act Notice: This information is to be used by the agency collecting it or its assignees in determining whether you qualify as a prospective mortgagor under its program. It will not be disclosed outside the agency except as required and permitted by law. You do not have to provide this information, but if you do not your application for approval as a prospective mortgagor or borrower may be delayed or rejected. The information requested in this form is authorized by Title 38, USC, Chapter 37 (if VA); by 12 USC, Section 1701 et. seq. (if HUD/FHA); by 42 USC, Section 1452b (if HUD/CPD); and Title 42 USC, 1471 et. seq., or 7 USC, 1921 et. seq. (if USDA/FmHA).

Instructions:
Lender - Complete items 1 through 7. Have applicant(s) complete item 8. Forward directly to donor listed in item 1.
Donor - Please complete items 9 through 17 as applicable and return directly to lender named in item 2.
Depository - Please complete items 18 through 24 and return to lender in item 2.
The form is to be transmitted directly to the lender and is not to be transmitted through the applicant(s) or any other party.

Part I - Request

1. To (Name and address of donor)	2. From (Name and address of lender)

I certify that this verification has been sent directly to the donor and has not passed through the hands of the applicant or any other party.

3. Signature of Lender	4. Title	5. Date	6. Loan Number (Optional)

7. Name of Applicant(s) and Property Address	8. Signature of Applicant(s)
	X
	X

We have been advised that you are the donor of a monetary gift to the applicant(s) for the purpose of a home purchase. Please complete Part II below.

Part II - To be Completed by Donor

9. Dollar Amount of Gift	10. Donor's Phone Number	11. Relationship to Applicant(s)

12. Donor's Statement and Signature

I/We state that no repayment of this gift is expected.

_____ (Signature)   _____ (Signature)

Signed and sworn before me

(date)   _____ (Notary Public)

13. ☐ Funds have been transferred to applicant(s)   ☐ Funds currently held in my account
Date Transferred:

14. Name of Donor's Depository	15. Account Number

16. Address of Depository	17. Authorization to Verify this Information
	(signature)

Part III - To be Completed by Depository

18. Account Number	19. Current Balance

Part IV — Authorized Signature - Federal statutes provide severe penalties for any fraud, intentional misrepresentation, or criminal connivance or conspiracy purposed to influence the issuance of any guaranty or insurance by the VA Secretary, the USDA, FmHA/FHA Commissioner, or the HUD/CPD Assistant Secretary.

20. Signature of Depository Representative	21. Title (Please print or type)	22. Date

23. Print or type name signed in Item 20

24. Phone No.

6/91

FE-40G

VMP -40G (9106).02 VMP MORTGAGE FORMS • (800)521-7291

DONOR/DEPOSITORY-RETURN BOTH COPIES TO LENDER

59

<u>Request for Verification of Employment (VOE)</u>

The VOE is sent for the same purpose as the VOM and VOD. The VOE goes to present and previous employers to confirm your employment history and income.

FannieMae — Request for Verification of Employment

Privacy Act Notice: This information is to be used by the agency collecting it or its assignees in determining whether you qualify as a prospective mortgagor under its program. It will not be disclosed outside the agency except as required and permitted by law. You do not have to provide this information, but if you do not your application for approval as a prospective mortgagor or borrower may be delayed or rejected. The information requested in this form is authorized by Title 38, USC, Chapter 37 (if VA); by 12 USC, Section 1701 et. seq. (if HUD/FHA); by 42 USC, Section 1452b (if HUD/CPD); and Title 42 USC, 1471 et. seq., or 7 USC, 1921 et. seq. (if USDA/FmHA).

Instructions: Lender - Complete items 1 through 7. Have applicant complete item 8. Forward directly to employer named in item 1.
Employer - Please complete either Part II or Part III as applicable. Complete Part IV and return directly to lender named in item 2.
The form is to be transmitted directly to the lender and is not to be transmitted through the applicant or any other party.

Part I — Request

1. To (Name and address of employer)	2. From (Name and address of lender)

I certify that this verification has been sent directly to the employer and has not passed through the hands of the applicant or any other interested party.

3. Signature of Lender	4. Title	5. Date	6. Lender's Number (Optional)

FOLD

I have applied for a mortgage loan and stated that I am now or was formerly employed by you. My signature below authorizes verification of this information.

7. Name and Address of Applicant (include employee or badge number)	8. Signature of Applicant
	X

Part II — Verification of Present Employment

9. Applicant's Date of Employment	10. Present Position	11. Probability of Continued Employment

12A. Current Gross Base Pay (Enter Amount and Check Period)

Annual Weekly Other (Specify)
Monthly Hourly

$

13. For Military Personnel Only

Pay Grade

14. If Overtime or Bonus is Applicable, Is Its Continuance Likely?
Overtime Bonus
Yes No Yes No

12B. Gross Earnings

Type	Year To Date	Past Year 19____	Past Year 19____
Base Pay	Thru_____ 19_____ $	$	$
Overtime	$	$	$
Commissions	$	$	$
Bonus	$	$	$
Total	$	$	$

Type	Monthly Amount
Base Pay	$
Rations	$
Flight or Hazard	$
Clothing	$
Quarters	$
Pro Pay	$
Overseas or Combat	$
Variable Housing Allowance	$

15. If paid hourly — average hrs. per wk.

16. Date of applicant's next pay increase

17. Projected amount of next pay increase

18. Date of applicant's last pay increase

19. Amount of last pay increase

20. Remarks (If employee was off work for any length of time, please indicate time period and reason)

FOLD

Part III — Verification of Previous Employment

21. Date Hired	23. Salary/Wage at Termination Per (Year) (Month) (Week)
22. Date Terminated	Base_____ Overtime_____ Commissions _____ Bonus_____
24. Reason for Leaving	25. Position Held

Part IV — Authorized Signature
Federal statutes provide severe penalties for any fraud, intentional misrepresentation, or criminal connivance or conspiracy purposed to influence the issuance of any guaranty or insurance by the VA Secretary, the USDA, FmHA/FHA Commissioner, or the HUD/CPD Assistant Secretary.

26. Signature of Employer	27. Title (Please print or type)	28. Date

29. Print or type name signed in Item 26

30. Phone No.

Fannie Mae
Form 1005 Mar. 90

FE-40

EMPLOYER-RETURN BOTH COPIES TO LENDER

61

<u>Statement of Purpose for Refinance</u>

This is one that you write. A simple statement of purpose is sufficient. "To get a lower rate and a lower payment" or something similar will serve if you are not taking money out of the new loan. If you are taking money from the refinancing-say, for remodeling or debt consolidation-explain where monies are to go. You may be asked to provide contractors' bids for remodeling. Make sure you sign the statement

The purpose for our finance request is ...

_____

_____

_____

_____

_____

_____

_____

_____

_____

_____

_____

_____

_____

<u>Fair Lending Notice</u>

This document confirms that the decision to extend credit is not to be based on race, religion, color, sex, marital status, national origin, or ancestry. It also indicates where any complaints you may have should be directed.

THE HOUSING FINANCIAL DISCRIMINATION ACT OF 1977

FAIR LENDING NOTICE

IT IS ILLEGAL TO DISCRIMINATE IN THE PROVISION OF OR IN THE AVAILABILITY OF FINANCIAL ASSISTANCE BECAUSE OF THE CONSIDERATION OF:

1. TRENDS, CHARACTERISTICS OR CONDITIONS IN THE NEIGHBORHOOD OR GEO-GRAPHIC AREA SURROUNDING A HOUSING ACCOMMODATION, UNLESS THE FI-NANCIAL INSTITUTION CAN DEMONSTRATE IN THE PARTICULAR CASE THAT SUCH CONSIDERATION IS REQUIRED TO AVOID AN UNSAFE AND UNSOUND BUSINESS PRACTICE; OR
2. RACE, COLOR, RELIGION, SEX, MARITAL STATUS, NATIONAL ORIGIN OR ANCESTRY.

3. QUEST FINANCIAL GROUP, INC. AS PART OF PROCESSING YOUR LOAN APPLICATION FOR A REAL ESTATE LOAN, HAS OR WILL REQUEST A CONSUMER REPORT BEARING ON YOUR CREDIT WORTHINESS, CREDIT STANDING AND CREDIT CAPACITY. THIS NOTICE IS GIVEN PURSUANT TO THE FAIR CREDIT REPORTING ACT OF 1970, SECTION 622, INCLUSIVE. YOU ARE ENTITLED TO SUCH INFORMATION WITHIN 60 DAYS OF WRITTEN DEMAND, THEREFORE, MADE TO THE CREDIT REPORTING AGENCY, PURSUANT TO SECTION 606 (b) OF THE FAIR CREDIT REPORTING ACT.

IT IS ILLEGAL TO CONSIDER THE RACIAL, ETHNIC, RELIGIOUS OR NATIONAL ORIGIN COMPOSITION OF A NEIGHBORHOOD OR GEOGRAPHIC AREA SURROUNDING A HOUSING ACCOMMODATION OR WHETHER OR NOT SUCH COMPOSITION IS UNDERGOING CHANGE, OR IS EXPECTED TO UNDERGO CHANGE, IN APPRAISING A HOUSING ACCOMMODATION OR IN DETERMINING WHETHER OR NOT, OR UNDER WHAT TERMS AND CONDITIONS, TO PROVIDE FINANCIAL ASSISTANCE.

THESE PROVISIONS GOVERN FINANCIAL ASSISTANCE FOR THE PURPOSE OF THE PURCHASE, CONSTRUCTION, REHABILITATION OR REFINANCING OF ONE TO FOUR UNIT FAMILY RESIDENCES OCCUPIED BY THE OWNER AND FOR THE PURPOSE OF THE HOME IMPROVEMENT OF ANY ONE TO FOUR UNIT FAMILY RESIDENCE.

IF YOU HAVE QUESTIONS ABOUT YOUR RIGHTS, OR IF YOU WISH TO FILE A COMPLAINT, CONTACT THE MANAGEMENT OF THIS FINANCIAL INSTITUTION OR:

DEPARTMENT OF REAL ESTATE   DEPARTMENT OF REAL ESTATE
107 SOUTH BROADWAY   185 BERRY STREET
ROOM 8107   ROOM 5816
LOS ANGELES, CA 90012   SAN FRANCISCO, CA 94107

NOTICE TO APPLICANT
IN ACCORDANCE WITH EQUAL CREDIT OPPORTUNITY ACT (ECOA)

THE FEDERAL EQUAL OPPORTUNITY ACT PROHIBITS CREDITORS FROM DISCRIMINATION AGAINST CREDIT APPLICANTS ON THE BASIS OF RACE, COLOR, RELIGION, NATIONAL ORIGIN, SEX, MARITAL STATUS, AGE (PROVIDED THE APPLICANT HAS THE CAPACITY TO ENTER INTO A BINDING CONTRACT); BECAUSE ALL OR PART OF THE APPLICANT'S INCOME DERIVES FROM ANY PUBLIC ASSISTANCE PROGRAMS; OR BECAUSE THE APPLICANT HAS IN GOOD FAITH EXERCISED ANY RIGHT UNDER THE CONSUMER CREDIT PROTECTION ACT. THE FEDERAL AGENCY THAT ADMINISTERS COMPLIANCE WITH THE LAW CONCERNING THIS CREDITOR IS THE FEDERAL LOAN BANK BOARD, 600 CALIFORNIA STREET, P.O. BOX 7948, SAN FRANCISCO, CALIFORNIA 94120.

INCOME RECEIVED FROM ALIMONY, CHILD SUPPORT, OR SEPARATE MAINTENANCE NEED NOT BE REVEALED UNLESS YOU CHOOSE SUCH SOURCES TO BE CONSIDERED AS A BASIS FOR REPAYING THIS OBLIGATION. INCOME FROM THESE SOURCES AS WELL AS ANY OTHER SOURCE, INCLUDING PART-TIME OR TEMPORARY EMPLOYMENT WILL NOT BE DISCOUNTED BY THE LENDER BECAUSE OF YOUR SEX, OR MARITAL STATUS; HOWEVER, THE LENDER WILL CONSIDER CAREFULLY THE STABILITY OF ALL INCOME YOU DISCLOSE.

ACKNOWLEDGMENT OF RECEIPT

I (WE) RECEIVED A COPY OF THIS NOTICE.

_____   _____
APPLICANT SIGNATURE   DATE   APPLICANT SIGNATURE   DATE

65

Federal Truth-in-Lending Disclosure Statement

One form that you will be receiving-perhaps more than one-is the TIL disclosure. The document (referred to as Reg. Z for the establishing regulation) is issued three days after an application is taken or three days after a broker has submitted a loan to an investor. Lenders are required to provide you an estimate of your annual percentage rate and amount financed. Please note that this is just an estimate. You should also be aware that you might receive one from your broker and then another one from the specific lender. Don't panic if the figures don't match. The forms are computer generated, using different assumed factors. Lenders use their own factors, which means that the figures will be different.

The example shown is for a 30-year loan of $50,000 written at an interest rate of 7.625%. Some key items to note that often cause confusion are the following.

A. The annual percentage rate represents the cost of the loan for the first year expressed as an interest rate. This simply means that although the interest rate is 7.625%, when costs are added; the actual rate is in excess of 8%. You need to be aware of this because several lenders advertise a low rate of 3%, but show an APR of 6%, which suggests that there may be some hidden costs.

B. Finance charges are best understood by looking at the total of payments (d) and subtracting the amount financed (c) to arrive at the interest charged for the loan.

C. The amount financed will generally be different from the loan amount. On a loan of $50,000, a figure of $47,157.30 would suggest closing costs of $2,842.70. If the lender promised that your payment would never change from $353.90 (f) and your APR was 8.166%, then working the number backwards would mean that your loan would have to be roughly $47,157 or the amount shown in box c.

D. To calculate the total number of payments, simply multiply the monthly payment by the number of months of the loan.

E. In a purchase, this figure will include your down payment and represent your total sales price.

F. The amount of the monthly payment you will make as pre-calculated, using the loan amount, the rate, and the number of months. There is generally one smaller payment at the end to adjust the distribution of interest and principal to the total loan.

FEDERAL TRUTH-IN-LENDING DISCLOSURE STATEMENT
(MADE IN COMPLIANCE WITH FEDERAL LAW)

Lender:

Borrower:

Loan No. 93-7-913

Property Address:

Date: 10/11/93

[X] Initial disclosure at time of application   [ ] Final disclosure based on contract terms

ANNUAL PERCENTAGE RATE The cost of your credit as a yearly rate.	FINANCE CHARGE The dollar amount the credit will cost you assuming the annual percentage rate does not change.	Amount Financed The amount of credit provided to you or on your behalf.	Total of Payments The amount you will have paid after you have made all payments as scheduled assuming the annual percentage rate does not change.	Total Sale Price The total cost of your purchase on credit, including your downpayment of:
A	B	C	D	E
E 8.166 %	E 80242.70	E 47157.30	E 127400.00	E 80242.70

Your payment schedule will be:

NUMBER OF PAYMENTS	* AMOUNT OF PAYMENTS	WHEN PAYMENTS ARE DUE MONTHLY BEGINNING	NUMBER OF PAYMENTS	* AMOUNT OF PAYMENTS	WHEN PAYMENTS ARE DUE MONTHLY BEGINNING
359	353.90 F	12/01/1993			
1	349.90	11/01/2023			

* Includes mortgage insurance premiums, excludes taxes, hazard insurance or flood insurance.

[X] **DEMAND FEATURE:** This loan transaction [ ] does [X] does not have a demand feature.

[X] **REQUIRED DEPOSIT:** The annual percentage rate does not take into account your required deposit.

[ ] **VARIABLE RATE FEATURE:** The annual percentage rate may increase during the term of your loan if the index used to set the Note interest rate increases. A new index may be substituted under certain circumstances and substitution of the new index may also increase the rate. The index at the beginning of your loan is described below:

[ ] This transaction is subject to a variable rate feature and is secured by your principal dwelling. Variable rate disclosures have been provided at an earlier time.

SECURITY INTEREST: You are giving a security interest in:

[X] the goods or property being purchased.

[ ]

FILING OR RECORDING FEES $ 50

LATE CHARGE: If a payment is more than   15   days late, you will be charged $ 17.69 / 5   % of the principal and interest past due.

PREPAYMENT: If you pay off your loan early, you

[ ] may   [X] will not have to pay a penalty.

[X] may   [ ] will not be entitled to a refund of part of the finance charge.

INSURANCE: Credit life, accident health or loss of income insurance is not required in connection with this loan. This loan transaction requires the following property insurance:

[X] Hazard Insurance   [ ] Flood Insurance   [ ] Private Mortgage Insurance

Borrower(s) may obtain property insurance through any person of his/her choice provided said carrier meets the requirements of the lender.

ASSUMPTION: If this loan is to purchase and is secured by your principal dwelling, someone buying your principal dwelling,

[ ] may   [X] may, subject to conditions   [ ] may not   assume the remainder of your loan on the original terms.

See your contract documents for additional information regarding nonpayment, default, right to accelerate the maturity of the obligation, prepayment rebates and penalties, and the Lender's policy regarding assumption of the obligation.

[X] check boxes where applicable

[X] all dates and numerical disclosures except late payment disclosures are estimates.   E means an estimate

"The undersigned hereby acknowledge receiving and reading a completed copy of this disclosure along with copies of the documents provided. The delivery and signing of this disclosure does not constitute an obligation on the part of the lender to make or the Borrower(s) to accept the loan as identified."

67

Fee Letter

Often, the borrower pays for some items such as credit report and appraisal before a loan approval is issued. This is especially frequent when an outside vendor such as an appraiser charges a broker. Very often, the broker because of daily cash flow finds it difficult to pay on the borrowers behalf. Instead, the broker simply collects a predetermined amount and ensures that the appraiser is paid. This is often a request made by an appraiser since so much work is conducted before a borrower commits. This approach eliminates anyone left "holding the bill" in the event a borrower changes their mind after work has been done and before monies can be collected. The Fee Letter lists those expenses and serves as a receipt for any that you pay.

FEE LETTER

To our client,

In order to process your loan application it is necessary for
Quest Financial Group, Inc., to incur certain expenses.
Therefore, it is necessary for us to collect the following fees
in advance:

       Personal credit report (e) $_____

       Business credit report (e)   _____

       Appraisal fee   (e)   _____

       Miscellaneous   _____

       TOTAL DUE $_____

Please remit the sum of $ _____ to Quest Financial
Group, Inc., for the above requested fees.

In addition, it is understood and agreed to that these fees are
NON-REFUNDABLE.

Quest Financial Group, Inc.

Borrower _____ Date _____

Borrower _____ Date _____

Borrower _____ Date _____

Borrower _____ Date _____

69

ARM Consumer Handbook Affidavit

When adjustable rate mortgages became popular, borrowers-in part naively and in part beguiled by smoothly-talking lenders-knew that payments could go up, but they didn't expect them to. Some borrowers were quite shocked when they received their first notice of increase. There were also complaints about the ways that banks and S&L's assessed and handled the increases.

To avoid such surprises and complaints, the Federal Home Loan Bank Board requires that all borrowers receive a handbook that explains the way that ARMs work. To protect themselves, lenders ask borrowers to sign a statement that they have read and reviewed the handbook before applying for an ARM. As much as one might resist reading such material and as easy as it is to sign the document while saying to oneself, "I know what an ARM is," you owe it to yourself to be sure. Read the handbook and ask about any aspect that is not clear.

ARM CONSUMER HANDBOOK AFFIDAVIT

To our client,

RE: Federal Home Loan Bank Board Regulations Requiring Dissemination of Consumer Handbooks on Adjustable Rate Mortgages.

I/We certify that I/We have received and reviewed a copy of the Consumer Handbook on Adjustable Rate Mortgages prior to making application for an adjustable rate loan."

Borrower_____   Date_____

Borrower_____   Date_____

Borrower_____   Date_____

Borrower_____   Date_____

71

Reading a Credit Report

One of the first actions of a loan processor is to get your credit history from which an underwriter can review your credit habits. First let's look at a sample of a credit report from one company. Please note that just like the Good Faith Estimate, the credit report comes in a variety of formats. (More on that later.) The general information is the same on all reports.

Much of the credit report is self-explanatory, but it is worth going over the section headed "CREDIT HISTORY" and reviewing first the columns and then the entries below the columns.

CREDITOR: The name of the person or creditor from whom you have received credit. Sometimes the credit report does not provide this information. It is then the job of the processor to obtain the information needed to confirm your credit rating. Below the name of the creditor is the account number. Of course, you will have all your account numbers clearly written for the taking of your loan application. That will mean that any discrepancy or confusion on your credit report can be more easily cleared (which you will probably take care of yourself if you order a credit report before the process starts). If there are unfamiliar accounts on your report, or if you have a checking account, a savings account, an auto loan, a personal loan, and a credit card, all with one bank or credit union, you'll find that account numbers are the means for unraveling mysteries.

ECOA: Equal Credit Opportunity Act: The letters in this column simply indicate whether the account belongs to the borrower ("B"), the co-borrower ("C"), or is a joint account ("J").

DATE OPENED: Date the account became active. An underwriter uses the date to help determine your level of experience with the use of credit. A very recently opened account does not tell much about paying habits.

DATE LAST REPORTED: Establishes current status of the account. For accounts that have been paid in full, the date shown (month and year) tells something about your promptness or consistency of paying. For current accounts, the date would ordinarily be a month or two earlier than the date of the report. If there hasn't been a report for several months, the matter should be checked.

PREPARED FOR	NURSERY RHYME MORTGAGE	ATTENTION	LITTLE RED	ACCOUNT #	100
LOAN TYPE	CONVENTIONAL	DATE RECEIVED	10-13-89	DATE COMPLETED	10-13-89
COMMENTS	BUYER INTERVIEWED 10-13-89			AUTHENTICATION	11111

CHARGES $ 0.00
00030204

BORROWER	CO-BORROWER

BORROWER'S NAME WATERS, JACK	CO-BORROWER'S NAME WATERS, JILL
STREET ADDRESS 12345 UPHILL LANE	
CITY, STATE, ZIP BROKEN CROWN, CA 90000	
BORROWER'S S.S. # 000-11-0000 AGE 35	CO-BORROWER'S S.S. # 000-22-0000 AGE 35
MARITAL STATUS MARRIED LENGTH OF TIME MARRIED N/A	RECORD OF SEPARATION OR DIVORCE NONE DISCLOSED
DEPENDENTS OTHER THAN BORROWER AND SPOUSE THREE	AGES 3, 2, 1, YEARS

EMPLOYMENT

B-EMPLOYER PURRELESS WATER	CB-EMPLOYER RAGING WATERS
POSITION HELD PURIFIER SINCE 7-85	POSITION HELD LIFE PRESERVER SINCE 7-85
VERIFIED BY MR. TASTE INCOME 2500. MO	VERIFIED BY SUSIE SAFETY INCOME 1500. MO
PERSONNEL EST.	MANAGER EST.

EMPLOYMENT HISTORY

B-PREVIOUS: TOWN CRIER, 6-83 TO 6-85, WEE WILLIE WINKLE, INC.
C-PREVIOUS: BABY SITTER, 12-84 TO 6-85, MOTHERS BEACH.

RESIDENCE HISTORY

CURRENT: SUBJ STATES BUYING FOR 1.5 YEARS, PAYING $700. PER MONTH.
PREVIOUS: 54321 DOWNHILL LANE, TUMBLE, CA; RENTED 2 YEARS.

REPOSITORIES ACCESSED   TU & TRW S/W   MU: JM RT: JM OC: JM SUPP:

73

CREDIT HISTORY												
CREDITOR	E C O A	DATE OPENED	DATE LAST REPORTED	HIGH CREDIT	APPROX. BALANCE	PAYMENT TERMS	30-59	60-89	90+	DATE LAST PAST DUE	PAYING RECORD	# OF MOS. REV
HUBBARD S&L		BY MAIL ONLY SUPPLEMENT TO FOLLOW										
B OF A VISA	C	2-82	4-89	1000.	495.	REV	0	0	0		AS AGREED	
143000047000												
PENNEYS	J	3-79	3-89	500.	320.	REV	0	0	0		AS AGREED	
51285067												
SAKS	B	7-80	3-89	500.	-0-	REV	0	0	0		AS AGREED	
18976453												
SEARS	J	3-81	4-89	1000.	-0-	INST	1	0	0		CURRENT	
345679021												
SEC PAC NATL BK	J	8-85	3-88	2500.	-0-	PAID	0	0	0		AS AGREED	
NORDSTROM	J	6-83	5-89	800.	145.	UNPAID COLLECTION ACCOUNT						
7689476574		(714-555-1212 SUSIE)										
HOME S&L	J	2-87	7-89	50000.	48000.	360@ 140.	0	0	0		AS AGREED	24
123456789000												

INQUIRIES: NONE WITHIN PAST 90 DAYS

PUBLIC RECORD: NONE OF RECORD THIS DATE TO REPORT

OTHER INCOME: SUBJECT STATES RECEIVES $350. PER MONTH RENTAL INCOME.

ADDITIONAL INFORMATION: ECOA KEY: B=BORROWER C=CO-BORROWER J=JOINT
                            ** END OF REPORT **

HIGH CREDIT: The maximum amount the creditor allowed. If a real estate loan started at $150,000, that is the highest credit on that account. For department stores and credit cards the high credit if the limit set on your charge card: $1,000, $5,000. High credit figures tell the underwriter how much credit other people have been willing to extend to you and, therefore, something about your credit worthiness. Comparing the balance to the high credit for a real estate loan tells whether you have been paying on schedule. For revolving accounts, the balance tells something about the way you use credit.

APPROX. BALANCE: Balance due on the account on the date last reported. The figure will be used to calculate your overall debt structure. Because of the lag time in creditors' reporting of payments, recent payments may not be reflected in the credit report. Depending on how critical those payments are to your credit picture, you may want to contact the creditor or the reporting company or provide copies of cancelled checks-another reason for ordering a copy of your credit report.

PAYMENT TERMS: The repayment structure agreed upon. "REV" in that column indicates a revolving line of credit such as a credit card or department store account. There is no set payment amount. Payments are based on the balance due. (When you are preparing for the loan application, use the amount of your last payment, but note that if you just charged a $2,000 television set, your new balance will call for a higher payment, a matter of interest to lenders.)

Two numbers identify installment debts such as home, student, automobile loans, the specified payment amount and the number of months payments are to be made. A five-year car loan with a $125 payment, for example, is shown as 60 @ $125.

HISTORICAL STATUS: A listing of late payments. The numbers at the top ("30-59," "60-89," and "90+") indicate how late. The numbers in the column indicate how many times you were late. A "1" under "90+" indicates one payment that was over 90 days late. A "Y' under "30-59" indicates that three payments were at least 30 days late. Very many of those numbers create an unfavorable picture for future borrowing; obviously, you want nothing but zeroes in this column. The derogatory entries are generally followed by the specific date so that you can compare your records with the report.

A new account is generally identified as "Too New To Rate."

PAYING RECORD: A summary comment regarding the way payments have been made. Notice that the easiest section to read on this credit report is an uninterrupted string of "AS AGREED" entries. Lenders' eyes can't miss that succession. It says that the borrower is responsible; that the borrower pays contracted debts. If anything can offset a high debt to income ratio, it is a spotless paying record. Conversely, imagine a few derogatory comments such as "UNSATISFACTORY" interrupting the favorable comments. The picture of the borrower changes. The borrower loses the impact of the repetition of the same favorable words.

For loans that have been paid off, the word "paid" appears. Derogatory comments such as "Paid Charge Off, Collection" may appear in this column.

Such comments make it much less likely that lenders will extend further credit. Your loan processor will ask you to provide a written letter of explanation and perhaps supporting documents. Don't panic. With those explanations, many such comments can be accepted as isolated incidents.

As noted above, there are things that can be done about "derogs." Level with your loan agent. Only when the loan agent knows the facts can he/she make the best recommendations.

75

NOTE: There may have been a time when one could be rather casual about paying bills from dentists, doctors, department stores, telephone companies, utilities companies, and others. Being an established customer seemed to be what mattered. Today, the delinquent notices arrive much more quickly. While it may be simpler to pay all bills on the first of the month, it may be more advisable to note due dates and mail payments early enough to beat those due dates.

 # OF MOS. REVIEWED: The number of months of payments reviewed on that account for this report. Generally, all accounts must be reviewed for at least 12 months. Creditors do not always provide this information. It is, therefore, possible that you will be asked to provide 12 months of cancelled checks to establish that your payments were made on time. You will need to copy both sides of those checks.

INQUIRES: (*First item under the columns just explained.*) Record of requests for your credit report. Every time anyone asks for your credit report, the request is noted. Sometimes you may be unaware that the request was made, or you may not remember just what companies you allowed to request reports when you were shopping for an auto loan, or you may forget that you signed one of those offers for a marvelous credit card.

Lenders get suspicious about those requests, especially if they are from other lenders. The requests may indicate that some other tender turned you down or that there is a problem with your credit. You will probably be asked to explain, which you can usually do easily. If, for example, while you were shopping for a lender or a mortgage company, a loan broker told you that he could give you much better advice if you spent $10 for a preliminary report and you did so but chose to use the current lender and never had the discussion with the broker, all you need to do is write a To Whom It May Concern note. What the lender wants to know is that an inquiry did not lead to some undisclosed financial obligation.

PUBLIC RECORD: Listing of any judgment or tax lien by the city or state or a mechanic's lien. In most cases, any outstanding obligations will need to be, cleared before credit is issued.

OTHER INCOME: What you have previously reported as other income. Go back to the earlier treatment of "other income" to check your documentation of any such income. Documentation can be attached to the current loan application or given to the loan processor as soon as available.

#22 HELPFUL HINT: Investigate carefully, advertisements that offer a quick and complete repair of your credit record. You may pay for doing things that you can take care of yourself. Use such a service only when you have established that the advertiser does give value for cost.

It was stated earlier that credit reports present similar information in various forms. Strictly speaking, what we have been looking at is an "in file" tri-merge report. A credit report is a single report generated by a firm such as TRW (Experian). A TRW report is generated from the repository of information at TRW. A tri-merge report is generated from more than one repository and, therefore, provides a better picture of your history; items not in one repository may be in another. Tri-merge reports include public record information, for example, which credit reports do not. Of course, pulling information from more that one repository means that reports cost more to prepare. The most popular repositories along with Experian are Trans Union and Equifax.

Any credit report you can order will be useful for pulling your information together for the loan application. It does take a few minutes to learn to read a report with which you are not familiar, ask your loan agent about any items or entries that are not clear.

NOTE: A *personal* credit report will be obtained for any applicant for a real estate loan Sometimes it is necessary to review the credit history of a business. For that, a business report is generated.

A bit more on credit reports before we go. Credit scoring has become very important to lenders in assessing borrowers credit worthiness. As one might suspect the higher the score the better credit risk. Conversely, the lower the score the poorer the risk you are likely to be. Why should you care? Well very often the score you have will dictate the credit class you will be assigned and ultimately the cost you will pay for your loan in interest rate or even in the amount of loan you may borrower. It's time to introduce "Fair Isaac Company" to you. Who Fair Isaac is, is not important and more information can be found by visiting the library. However, what is important is that they have established the rules and standards that many lenders follow as to credit risk evaluation. Lenders refer this score as a FICO score. Scores can range from as low as 300 and as high as 900 during the time this book was written. To make things more complete, each repository mentioned earlier has their own FICO scoring system so it is very likely that one borrower may have 3 different scores to contend with. For example a borrower with good credit might have scores something like 685,702,710. In many cases, the lender might throw out the high and the low and keep the middle. Like they do in many Olympic sporting events.

77

What should you take from this segment about FICO scoring? Well, simply that credit decisions are often based on your credit score. Typically scores are made up from factors which include your past payment performance, credit utilization, credit history, types of credit in use, and the number of inquires. You should demand to know your scores when you talk to a lender and ask them how they chose the one they used.

#23 | HELPFUL HINT: Since FICO scoring is so important to your borrowing power, make sure you limit the number of people who have access to your credit. Remember, when shopping for a loan a lender will need to see your credit. When they pull your report, they are initiating an inquire. Even department store clerks who want to "give you" a new department store card will initiate an inquire. Too many inquires will negatively impact your score and hence your power. When you run your credit report, record your score. Then, when you are shopping for a loan tell the agent you have scores of 685,702, and 710. If they insist on running your report or tell you they can't give you a rate until they run your report, you may wish to consider finding another lender since this one may cause you more damage than good.

Appraising the Property

The lender wants to know the worth of the property that is to secure the loan. The loan agent calls an established, approved appraiser, probably someone the agent has worked with in the past. The appraiser prepares a report, estimating the value of the house, and the loan agent uses that report to support the loan request.

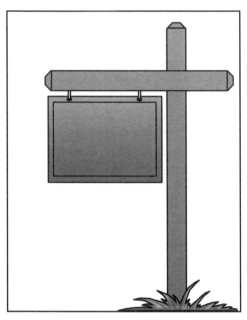

If you are refinancing, you will get a call from your loan agent or possibly from the appraiser to set a time for the appraisal. If you are buying a house, the call goes from the realtor to the seller; you're not involved. The appraiser goes to the property, takes measurements inside and out, takes pictures, and makes notes

78 throughout. (A "drive-by" appraisal may be adequate for some purposes.) After the visit, the appraiser searches records of houses in that area that has sold recently and chooses houses that are most closely comparable to the house being appraised. Details of those comparable houses (called "comps") are used to help establish a value for the property. The appraiser prepares a report showing the details of the property and the comps side-by-side and stating what the appraiser thinks the house is worth at that time.

Appraisers, who have individual ways of doing their work, spend only a few minutes at the property. One appraiser says that he is looking at the house and hardly sees furnishings or state of housekeeping but does notice the last-minute things-painting; watering-that the homeowner does to try to make the property look better. Another says that he spends hours trying to find the closest comps and lets the comps speak for the value of the house.

One homeowner says that the appraiser seemed to approach the job as if he were the one lending the money. Another homeowner, however, says that the appraiser seemed to want to help make the loan go through.

Appraising is variously called an art, a science, an educated guess, or a game. If several properties much like yours have recently sold in your area, the appraiser has fairly specific data to work with and can, methodically, scientifically, prepare a report quickly enough. If the appraiser can't find adequate comps, the task is more difficult, and the report may be delayed, possibly for weeks. More art than science is needed.

#24	HELPFUL HINT: A routine appraisal report can be completed in about a week, but appraisals have been known to take a month or two. If you are scheduling the appraiser's visit, you want the very first time the appraiser has available to get the process started in case there are any problems. Most loans can't be formally approved without the appraisal.

However the process is described, the appraisal report is a document recording the approximate market value of a property in a certain market at a given time. The report is specific to the time; a house can be appraised at one value today and at a different value two months from now.

#25	HELPFUL HINT: Remember the topic regarding FICO scores? Well FICO scores may impact whether or not your loan request requires an appraisal. Many loan products, especially second mortgage or equity loans allow a provision that states if you are requesting an amount of let's say less than $50,000 and you have a score above say 685, you may be exempt from a full appraisal. You may only require a "drive-by" where as the name implies, the appraiser simply drives by the property to make sure it exists or perhaps not even require that to be done. See how important credit management is?

In the mortgage world, there are two kinds of appraised values: Quick Sale Value (QSV) and Fair Market

Value (FMV). And there are two approaches to FMV: cost and market.

QUICK SALE VALUE	FAIR MARKET VALUE
	Cost Approach
	Market Approach

QSV is the approximate amount of money a property could generate in a forced sale, say within 90 days and without proper marketing. Quick sales are generally made when a bank has foreclosed on a property and wants to cut its losses.

A fair market value, on the other hand, takes into consideration adequate time for selling, proper marketing, the condition of the neighborhood, a willing seller, and a willing and able buyer.

FMV is what most lenders use and, therefore, what we are concerned with here. The cost approach to valuation computes the value of land and the replacement cost of improvements and depreciation. In other words, the value is what it would cost to rebuild the house at today's building costs.

The market approach to value is predicated upon actual prices paid in transactions in that market. It is a process of correlation and analysis of similar recently sold properties. In other words, the value is what other homes similar to yours sold for. Today, nearly all lending decisions are based on the market approach because it considers changing economic conditions more definitely than does the cost approach.

Because no two houses are entirely alike, adjustments are made to get the closest, comparison possible. Two houses in the same area may, for instance, have the same square footage, the same number of rooms, and other similar features except that the comp house has a swimming pool and the subject property does not. The appraiser subtracts the value of the pool from the selling price of the comp to make the comp more like the subject property. Conversely, if the subject property has the pool and the comp doesn't, the value of the pool is added to the comp to make it more like the subject property.

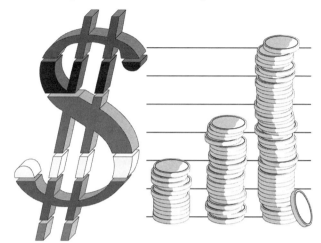

It may seem that the arithmetic is backward and that the value of the subject property should go up or down, but if you think about it for a while, you'll see that it works better to take the recently appraised and established value of the comp, up or down than to try to work with an unknown value of the subject property.

To give you a clearer picture of what the lender sees, let's take a partial look at a sample Uniform Residential Appraisal Report, one that shows both cost and market value. The numbered comments that follow refer to the numbered sections of the report. Perhaps you can look at those items now and then study the report in detail later.

81

Some items on the appraiser's report:

1. This section shows the cost approach. The numbers are construction costs in terms of square feet (at the time of the appraisal) and show the estimated cost of building the house.

2. **Subject property**, again, is the property being used as security.

3. An appraiser rates the general **condition** of a house, using a descriptive term such as "average" or "superior." Comp I is rated slightly superior to the subject property. The appraiser has, therefore, lowered the comp by $5,000 to reach a value closer to our subject.

4. For **Gross Living Area**, it is shown that the subject property is slightly larger in square footage than comp 2; the appraiser, therefore, estimates that an adjustment upward of $1000 to the comp would make it equal to the value of our subject.

5. and 6.   The comp had a value of **$300,000** (5) as of **1/19/93** (6), the date of the sale of the property. (The appraiser wants only recently established values.)

7. Considering the additional size and features of the comp, a **net (total) adjustment** of $38,000 downward was made on the comp to make it more like the subject.

8. That adjustment means that the appraiser's adjustment gives the comp an **indicated value** of $262,000, the figure that is to be used to help determine the value of the subject property.   All three comps and building costs are very close in this case, but if there were a wider spread of prices, this one higher value would be more important for getting the appraisal high enough to accommodate the requested loan.

9. The cost approach yields a value of $255,000. The average of all three comps after adjustments is $257,000. Given the **current market** and a willing buyer and seller, the appraiser concludes that the market value is $255,000.

The lender may or may not ask for a review of the appraisal. Anything unusual about the appraisal or the loan is, however, likely to call for a review. The review might simply add time to the process or might cause some problem to surface, a problem that would then have to be resolved.

UNIFORM RESIDENTIAL APPRAISAL REPORT   File No. 930515RT

Valuation Section

Purpose of Appraisal is to estimate Market Value as defined in Certification & Statement of Limiting Conditions.

BUILDING SKETCH (SHOW GROSS LIVING AREA ABOVE GRADE)	ESTIMATED REPRODUCTION COST - NEW - OF IMPROVEMENTS:		

If for Freddie Mac/Fannie Mae, show only square foot calculations & cost approach comments.

COST APPROACH

```
            x            x            =
            x            x            =
            x            x            =
            x            x            =
            x            x            =
            x            x            =
Total Gross Living Area                =
Functional Obsolescence        None
For
For
External    Obsolescence       None
For
For
The land /value rate is 58% which is typical of
this market area within this time period.
```

Dwelling 1,773 Sq. Ft. @ $ 70.00 = $ 124,110
Sq. Ft. @ $ =
Extras =
Special Energy Efficient Items None =
Porches, Patios, etc. Patio = 5,000
Garage/Carport 437 Sq. Ft. @ $ 35.00 = 15,295
Total Estimated Cost New = $ 144,405
Less   Physical | Functional | External
Depreciation 44,405 = $ 44,405
Depreciated Value of Improvements = $ 100,000
Site Imp. "as is" (driveway, landscaping, etc.) = $ 10,000
ESTIMATED SITE VALUE * = $ 145,000
(If leasehold, show only leasehold value.)
INDICATED VALUE BY COST APPROACH = $ 255,000   **1**

(Not Required by Freddie Mac and Fannie Mae)
Construction Warranty ☐ Yes ☒ No
Does property conform to applicable HUD/VA property standards? ☐ Yes ☐ No Name of Warranty Program N/A
If No, explain: _____   Warranty Coverage Expires N/A

The undersigned has recited three recent sales of properties most similar and proximate to subject and has considered these in the market analysis. The description includes a dollar adjustment, reflecting market reaction to those items of significant variation between the subject and comparable properties. If a significant item in the comparable property is superior to, or more favorable than, the subject property, a minus (-) adjustment is made, thus reducing the indicated value of subject; if a significant item in the comparable is inferior to, or less favorable than, the subject property, a plus (+) adjustment is made, thus increasing the indicated value of the subject.

SALES COMPARISON ANALYSIS

ITEM	SUBJECT	COMPARABLE NO. 1	+(-)$ Adjustment	COMPARABLE NO. 2	+(-)$ Adjustment	COMPARABLE NO. 3	+(-)$ Adjustment
Address	**2** 453 Santa Lucia Wood Hill	446 Canoga Dr. AP# 2190-001-02		220 Lopez St. AP# 2169-010-01		217 Ybarra Rd. AP# 2171-007-01	
Proximity to Subject		1 Strt. South 560-A5		3 Blks NW 560-A3		2 Sts. North 560-A5	
Sales Price	$ REFI	$ 275,000		$ 260,000		$ 300,000	**5**
Price/Gross Liv. Area	$ [7]	$ 139.81 [7]		$ 149.77 [7]		$ 150.15 [7]	
Data Source	Inspection	DataQuick/CMDC		DataQuick/CMDC		DataQuick/Title Co.	
VALUE ADJUSTMENTS	DESCRIPTION	DESCRIPTION	+(-)$ Adjustment	DESCRIPTION	+(-)$ Adjustment	DESCRIPTION	+(-)$ Adjustment
Sales or Financing Concessions		Conv. 90% Doc. 61632		Conv. 80% Doc# 62640		Conv. N/A Doc# 10931	
Date of Sale/Time	Current	04/01/93		03/15/93		01/19/93	**6**
Location	Good	Similar		Similar		Similar	
Site/View	5,040*/ None	9,000* /None		6,250* /None		13,900*/Prtl	-10,000
Design and Appeal	Ranch	Similar		Similar		Similar	
Quality of Construction	Average	Similar		Similar		Similar	
Age	1963	1967	**3**	1951		1964	
Condition	Average	Sl. Superior	-5,000	Sl. Superior	-5,000	Similar	
Above Grade	Total Bdrms Baths	Total Bdrms Baths		Total Bdrms Baths	**4**	Total Bdrms Baths	
Room Count	6 3 2	7 4 2		6 3 2		7 4 2.5	-2,000
Gross Living Area	1,773 Sq. Ft.	1,967 Sq. Ft.	-6,000	1,736 Sq. Ft.	+1,000	1,998 Sq. Ft.	-7,000
Basement & Finished Rooms Below Grade	None *Lt Ut 5,000	None *Lt Ut 9,000	-8,000	None *Lt Ut.6,250	-2,500	None *Lt Ut.7,000	-4,000
Functional Utility	Average	Similar		Similar		Similar	
Heating/Cooling	F.A.U./Cent.	F.A.U./Cent.		F.A.U./Cent.		F.A.U./Cent.	
Garage/Carport	2 Car Garage	2 Car Garage		2 Car Garage		2 Car Garage	
Porches, Patio, etc.	Patio	Similar		Similar		Similar	
Pools, etc.	No Pool/Spa	No Pool/Spa		No Pool/Spa		Pool & Spa	-15,000
Special Energy Efficient Items	None	None		None		None	
Fireplace(s)	1 Fireplace	1 Fireplace		1 Fireplace		1 Fireplace	
Other (e.g. kitchen equip., remodeling)	Fencing Built-ins	Fencing Built-ins		Fencing Built-ins		Fencing Built-ins	**7**
Net Adj. (total)		☐+ ☒- $	-19,000	☐+ ☒- $	-6,500	☐+ ☒- $	-38,000
Indicated Value of Subject		$ 256,000		$ 253,500		$ 262,000	**8**

Comments on Sales Comparison: _____ See Attached Addendum !!! _____

RECONCILIATION

INDICATED VALUE BY SALES COMPARISON APPROACH.......... $ 255,000

INDICATED VALUE BY INCOME APPROACH (If Applicable) Estimated Market Rent $ N/A /Mo. x Gross Rent Multiplier N/A = $ N/A

This appraisal is made ☒ "as is" ☐ subject to the repairs, alterations, inspections or conditions listed below ☐ completion per plans and specifications.

Comments and Conditions of Appraisal: Public records as reported by DataQuick, do not disclose a prior sale of the subject property within two years of the date of this appraisal, nor has it been listed.

Final Reconciliation: The Sale Comparison approach is considered to be the best indicator of value. The Cost Approach is weakened due to the difficulty in estimating accrued depreciation. The Income Approach is not considered applicable.

This appraisal is based upon the above requirements, the certification, contingent and limiting conditions, and Market Value definition that are stated in

☐ FmHA, HUD &/or VA instructions.
☒ Freddie Mac Form 439 (Rev.7/86) / Fannie Mae Form 1004B (Rev.7/86) filed with client _____ 19___ ☒ attached.

I (WE) ESTIMATE THE MARKET VALUE, AS DEFINED, OF THE SUBJECT PROPERTY AS OF 05 / 24 19 93 to be $ 255,000   **9**

I (We) certify: that to the best of my (our) knowledge and belief the facts and data used herein are true and correct; that I (we) personally inspected the subject property, both inside and out, have made an exterior inspection of all comparable sales cited in this report; and that I (we) have no undisclosed interest, present or prospective therein.

APPRAISER(S)
Signature _____   REVIEW APPRAISER (If applicable) Signature _____ ☐ Did ☒ Did Not Inspect Property
Name _____   Name _____

Freddie Mac Form 70 10/86 12 CPI   LaserJet Software by Dynamic Office Automation Inc. 1990   Fannie Mae Form 1004 10/86

83

Securing Title to the Property

If you have clear title to a property, you can sell it, trade it, keep it, make it an investment property, or borrow against your equity. If there is a cloud on the title (an easement, a judgment, or a lien), you can't do with the property as you wish. To make sure that no liens exist on the subject property, the loan processor orders a preliminary title report from a title company. The report reviews past ownership and shows a title history. The report is several pages long, but a typical page showing home ownership follows to give you some idea of what the report is like.

84

Usually the lender or broker selects a title company on your behalf, but you have the right to choose your own title company, which may save you money. Ask for price comparisons.

If it has been fewer than five years since you purchased or refinanced your home, you may be able to negotiate a "revamp fee" of 20% or more. A fee of $730 for title insurance for a $150,000 loan may be reduced to $580, for a savings of $150. (Not all title companies offer this feature.)

If you are refinancing your home with the same lender that holds your present mortgage, you may be entitled to a further discount.

You have the right to choose. Ask up front about some of these specials. If your broker or lender is not aware of them, ask about them yourself. It is your money. Many borrowers think that the cost of title insurance is definitely inflated, but, like life insurance, it has its purpose.

8. An easement for ingress and egress, road and public utility and incidental purposes, in favor of M.R.   as set forth in an instrument recorded February 24, 1970 in Book 36 , page 22 of Official Records, over the Easterly 16 feet of said land.

9. A Deed of Trust to secure an indebtedness in the original principal sum of $78,000.00, and any other amounts and/or obligations secured thereby, recorded March 24, 1987 as Document No. 87-04 65 of Official Records.
Loan Number: None Shown;
Dated: March 13, 1987;
Trustor: T. C. YOUNG and   N. B. YOUNG, husband and wife;
Trustee: CALIFORNIA   GENERAL   MORTGAGE   SERVICE,   INC.,   a corporation;
Beneficiary: NETWORK FUNDING CORPORATION, a California corporation.

The beneficial interest under said Deed of Trust was assigned by an assignment recorded May 18, 1987 as Document No. 87-076 4 of Official Records, to FEDERAL HOME LOAN MORTGAGE CORPORATION.

10. A Deed of Trust to secure an indebtedness in the original principal sum of $177,600.00, and any other amounts and/or obligations secured thereby, recorded October 17, 1989 as Document No. 89-1 6 05 of Official Records.
Loan Number: 1 674-2;
Dated: October 2, 1989;
Trustor: K. S.   NUT and   A.   NUT, husband and wife;
Trustee: ERRAN RECONVEYANCE COMPANY, a California corporation;
Beneficiary: SAVINGS OF AMERICA, F.A., a corporation.

11. A Deed of Trust to secure an indebtedness in the original principal sum of $22,200.00, and any other amounts and/or obligations secured thereby, recorded October 17, 1989 as Document No. 89-166006 of Official Records.
Loan Number: None Shown;
Dated: October 4, 1989;
Trustor: K. S.   NUT and   A.   NUT, husband and wife as joint tenants;
Trustee: COUNTY TRUST DEED CO., a California corporation;
Beneficiary: T. C.   YOUNG and   N. B. YOUNG, husband and wife as joint tenants.

Said Deed of Trust states it is second and subject to the Deed of Trust above mentioned.

85

<u>Preparing Yourself for Other Fees</u>

Processing your loan will produce other fees, and, even though you saw some of them on the Good Faith Estimate, you'll feel a slight - shock, we hope -when finally you see the settlement papers. To brace you for that shock, here is a list of closing costs. (Take some comfort: you won't have to pay all of them.)

APPRAISAL FEE: The money that pays an independent property appraiser for a statement of estimated property value.

APPRAISAL REVIEW FEE: A charge for review of the property appraisal to insure that it meets specific investor criteria.

ASSIGNMENT FEE: The charge a lender assesses to transfer, or assign, property rights or contract from one entity to another.

ASSUMPTION FEE: Administrative fee charged by the lender for preparation of legal documents that make it possible for a buyer to assume a loan.

CREDIT REPORT FEE: The cost of ordering the credit report.

DEMAND FEE: In a refinance, an administrative fee often charged by the existing lender to establish the most current loan balance and payoff figures, including any late charges, interest, or other costs or charges.

DOCUMENT FEE: The fee charged to cover the administrative cost of preparing legal papers, such as a mortgage, note, deed, or deed of trust.

ENDORSEMENT FEE: A charge from the title company for authenticating or endorsing any specific request made by a lender or other party. Examples include endorsements for flood certification, for environmental protection concerns, and for the salability of a loan.

ESCROW/SETTLEMENT FEE: An administrative fee paid to the closing agent for insuring the proper and unbiased execution of the transaction as instructed by all parties.

FLOOD CERTIFICATION FEE: A fee charged by an appraiser or lender to obtain proper flood zone verifications.

LOAN ORIGINATION FEE (POINTS): A one time charge by the lender which adjusts the yield on a loan to that which market conditions demand. Each point is equal to one percent of the mortgage amount.

LOAN TIE IN FEE: An additional administrative fee charged by' the closing agent to insure that all loan documents are properly prepared and are signed in the presence of the closing agent.

MESSENGER FEE: A service charge for mailing, shipping, or hand-delivery of any or all loan documents.

MORTGAGE INSURANCE PREMIUM: A fee paid at settlement for a policy, which protects the lender from loss resulting from default on payment, by the borrower.

NOTARY FEE: Fee paid to a licensed individual to affix his/her name and official seal to various documents to authenticate the execution of the documents by all participating parties.

PEST INSPECTION: Fee paid for inspection for termites or other pest infestations of the property.

PREPAID INTEREST: A charge paid at settlement for the interest that accrues on the mortgage from the date of settlement to the first regular monthly payment. The charge may be assessed on both a newly originated loan and an existing loan being paid in full.

PROCESSING FEE: Administrative costs incurred by the lender or broker in processing the loan.

RECONVEYANCE FEE: A fee charged by a title company, a new lender, or a previous lender who is being paid in full to record the reconveyance. (Often referred to as a "Forwarding Fee" or "Statement Fee.")

RECORDING FEE: A fee charged for legally recording a new deed and mortgage and collected any time a property changes ownership, a new mortgage loan is issued, or anything else pertaining to the transaction is recorded.

SUB ESCROW FEE: An administrative fee paid to the title company for insuring that all scheduled obligations are paid from loan proceeds. The fee is charged only when the title company handles money; it is not applicable to "all-cash" transactions.

TAX SERVICE CONTRACT: The lender's administrative cost for confirming whether or not property taxes have been paid.

TAX/INSURANCE IMPOUNDS: Funds held in an account by the lender to assure future payments of recurring items. The lender determines the amount that must be placed in reserve to pay the next insurance premium or property taxes when due and adds a prorated amount to monthly mortgage payments. It is often referred to as an escrow account.

TITLE INSURANCE: A one-time premium charged at settlement to protect a lender and/or borrower against losses that result from title defects.

UNDERWRITING FEE: A fee charged to offset the lender's administrative cost for analyzing credit, income, and collateral for reaching a loan decision.

WIRE TRANSFER FEE: A service fee charged by the lending institution of the newly originated mortgage to provide for the transfer of funds to a designated title company through the Federal Reserve or another service conduit.

Estimating Closing Costs

Although loan costs vary from loan to loan, you can make an estimate to determine whether the fees you are being quoted are reasonable. Study Appendix C, Table of Estimated Closing Costs, which shows fees for a loan at a 7.5% interest rate; then compare your quoted fees at your interest rate with the fees shown in the table.

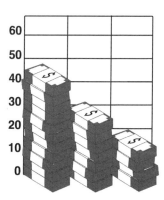

<u>Waiting for the Processing to End</u>

While your loan agent and loan processor are working on all those matters, you will be waiting. There are simply too many variables to say what is usual during this period. If any of the problems that have been mentioned develop, you may be busy working on them. You and your loan agent may be in touch often or infrequently. Approval may come in a few days, or it may take months. Waiting for it may be a casual interlude or a time of anxiety and frustration. Keeping the objective in mind (and not just the process) can make the waiting period pass more quickly and smoothly. If everything is working the way we all hope it will, the way we've been planning, you can relax about the processing and think about other things.

Remember that you have been through most of the twists and turns of the mortgage maze already. Take a deep breath and a relaxing pause before you enter the final stretch.

Chapter Five

Light at the End of the Tunnel:
Approving the Loan

Decision time.

When the loan agent and the loan processor conclude that they have a satisfactory loan application with adequate documentation, the loan agent sends the package to someone who can say yes or no on the loan. In a bank or savings bank, the application goes up the line to the loan committee. An application sent by a loan broker goes to a cooperating investor. In either case, technicians examine the arithmetic microscopically and cross check all the documentation. Then, using the technicians summary assessments, either a committee or an individual tests the package with the lender's criteria and makes a decision.

The Four Cs

The test can be put in terms of four words beginning with C.

· <u>C</u>redit: Will (does) the applicant pay debts?

· <u>C</u>apacity: Can the applicant pay this debt?

· <u>C</u>ollateral: Is the loan well covered by the value of the property?

· <u>C</u>ondition: What will the financial condition of the applicant be if the loan is made?

Mortgage professionals may add other C's such as <u>c</u>haracter or <u>c</u>ash, but we'll use these four.

Credit

To consider **credit**, to answer the question about willingness to pay, the underwriter studies your credit report and supporting documents, asking questions such as:

__How many other creditors have issued credit?
__How much credit has the applicant been issued in the past?
__How much experience has the applicant had using credit?
__What has been the history of repayment?
__How much of the available credit issued to the applicant is still available?
__Are there late payments? Why?
__Is there a strong and clear pattern of paying all debts?

From that study a picture emerges. If the picture is not clear, there may be a request; or explanation or more documentation.

Capacity

To consider **capacity**, to answer the question about the ability to pay, the underwriter studies your declaration of income and supporting documents, reducing all the figures to two ratios.

First, using the reported income that is acceptable, the monthly gross income is established. Then, a Front Housing Ratio (or front end ratio) is calculated. Housing costs (principal, interest, taxes, and insurance-abbreviated to PITI) are expressed as a percentage of gross monthly income. The acceptable maximum is ordinarily 28%.

Second, a Total Expense/Debt Ratio (commonly called back end ratio) is established. To the housing costs are added all other monthly obligations (installments, revolving debt, and so on). For total expense, an acceptable percentage of gross monthly income is 38%. (Some lenders may accept a higher figure with compensating factors and may or may not increase the interest rate or add points.)

The ratios for you are figured on the basis of debts you owe as established by the loan processor. By way of illustration, consider a computed gross income of $6,900 and debts as listed:

__New PITI payment	$1,750.00
__Car payment	325.00
__Revolving credit (all accounts)	350.00
TOTAL DEBT $2,425.00	

Housing costs are 25.36 % of monthly income, and all monthly obligations are 35.14%. Ratios would be written: 25.36/35.14. Those figures would indicate capacity to pay.

It was just indicated that all revolving credit accounts are counted. An installment debt with fewer than 10 months remaining, however, is generally not counted against the applicant.

#26 | HELPFUL HINT: If you have a car loan with 13 months left and a payment of $250, it may be worth paying $750 against your payments so that additional amount can reduce the term by 3 months and the debt can be eliminated based on the 10 month rule. Depending on your income, a $250 car payment could change your ratio from 40% to 38%, which could make a difference of 1/2% in fees or interest rate. On a loan of $150,000, that could be as much as $50 a month in payments or $750 in fees.

Don't panic if your ratios are higher. Remember, those are only generally acceptable figures. There are several lenders who specialize in loans with higher debt ratios. If you are working with a broker, the loan agent can switch immediately to a lender more likely to accept your numbers. Whoever the lender is, there is the same study of what you earn and what you owe.

From that study a picture emerges. If the picture is not clear, there may be a request for explanation or more documentation.

#27 | HELPFUL HINT: Here's a quick trick. If you're thinking of buying a home but don't know how much you can qualify for, try this approach. Take your monthly income and multiply it by 38%. From that number, subtract any installment debts and revolving credit card debt. Keeping mind that an underwriter will use 5 % of the credit card balance to formulate a monthly payment. That figure will represent the maximum PITI payment allowed. From that figure, subtract an extra $300 as an arbitrary, unscientific accounting for taxes and insurance, homeowners association fees, etc. Using the payment chart in Appendix A, find the going market interest rate and identify the closest monthly payment to the figure you calculated. Then find the corresponding loan amount. Within $1000 to $2000, that is a quick test to determine a loan amount you could qualify for. Add the monies you have available for a down payment, and you now have an approximate home value or sales price, which you can consider. Please note, that most ARM loans, despite a low start rate, will require qualification to be based on a rate of 7%. That will certainly make a difference if you make an error and base this approach on a start rate of 4%.

#28 | HELPFUL HINT: Here's a twist to this approach. Assume you know the loan amount you need and the corresponding monthly payment, but you're not sure you have the income to qualify. To the payment add any monthly debts and divide by 38%. That number is the income you would need to qualify for this size loan considering your total monthly debt. This twist works especially well if you happen to be a Real Estate agent trying to compute whether an individual can qualify to buy a particular home, given a particular payment.

Example 1:	Monthly income	$6100 X 38%	=	$2318
	Installment and credit debt		=	(625)
				$1693
	Taxes and Insurance			(300)
				$1393

95

Going market rate 7.5% 30 FRM
Closest payment per chart $1398

Maximum loan amount per chart $200,000

Example 2:	Assume $200,000 loan amount	
	Payment@ 7.5 %	$1398
	Misc. taxes & insurance	+300
	Misc. installment debt	+625
		$2323
	Divide by 38% (.38)	$6113
	Estimated income needed	**$6113**

Collateral

To consider collateral, to answer the question about the value of the property, the underwriter studies the appraisal and the loan.

If the facts the applicants present are inaccurate or misrepresented or if an underwriter miscalculates a ratio or income, the lender still has the value of the property to protect the money that funded the mortgage.

The lender is concerned about the loan-to-value (LTV) ratio.
If a house is appraised at $ 100,000 and the lender lends $ 100,000, the lender has no safeguards in case the borrower defaults on the loan. The lender also wants protection against declining market values, the borrower's failure to maintain the property, and the costs of holding and selling a foreclosed property. If the lender lends only $80,000 the lender has a margin of protection.

The lender, therefore, looks at the appraisal and, if there is one, the appraisal review. If the requested loan is no more than 80% of the appraised value, the lender is likely to consider that loan safe on an owner-occupied property. (Because the default rate is higher on non owner-occupied houses and because rental properties are not always well maintained, most lenders do not lend more than 75% on those properties.)

If the requested loan is more than 80% of the appraised value but the loan seems safe, the lender may make carrying Private Mortgage Insurance (PMI) a condition of funding the loan. PMI is a separate insurance policy, such as auto insurance, which protects the lender in the event you default on your payments. PMI is your cost, and the lender is the beneficiary. If a lender does not require PMI, there will probably be another fee to protect against loss.

#29 | HELPFUL HINT: If you are paying PMI, it is important that you keep track of your equity. When your loan balance decreases and the value of your property increases enough to drop the LTV below 80%, send a note to your lender requesting that you be exempt from PMI. If your payment history has been exemplary, the bank may grant your request. On a typical $150,000 loan, that could mean an annual savings of $500 to $600.

The higher the LTV, the more the lender has invested in the property and the less equity (the portion of the value of the house that is not encumbered) the buyer has in the property. Conversely, the lower the LTV, the less the lender has invested and the more equity the owner has. Loans with low LTV are, therefore, attractive to banks because there is a smaller investment. If you were to default, the bank could quickly sell the property, pay off the existing loan and miscellaneous costs, and take over your equity.

In many markets, property values have decreased. At the end of the 1980s and the beginning of the1990s, different parts of the country, first one and then another, experienced down turns in the economy and lower property values. Some parts of the country have begun seeing a return to better markets; some have not. In such markets the difference between what is owed and the value of the property is very small. Lenders are, therefore, much more likely to require PMI with new loans.

As a side note let's talk about portfolio lending. In short, portfolio lenders keep loans in their own portfolios rather than immediately to the secondary market Federal National Mortgage A (FNMA) or Federal Home Loan Mortgage Company (FHLM as most conventional lenders do. They have the ability, therefore, to create their own rules rather than follow those of others. The net result is that they may lend at higher LTV ratios than conventional lenders can without requiring PM That advantage notwithstanding, those portfolio lender limited in their product offerings and generally price their higher to compensate for the risk. This increase is often know insurance or as a stretch fee. Sometimes it is a better option PMI insurance than it is to obtain a loan without PMI from a lender. The point is, don't run to a company just becaus require PMI. Lenders watch rising and falling property values very closely and alter their lending practices to maximize the return on their investments. To protect your investment-your house-you, too, should be aware of its value.

#30 | HELPFUL HINT: County tax collectors send tax bills based on calculations that assume that property has appreciated in value. If, with two or three good comps, you can show that the value of your property has decreased, you can contact your county tax office and ask for a reassessment. You may save hundreds of dollars.

Your house is the collateral for your loan, and it is your home. For the lender, it is purely collateral. That is why the lender makes a thorough study of the appraisal and the loan that is requested. Emotional value, given by the owner, is not part of the appraisal.

From that study a picture emerges. If the picture is not clear, there may be a request for explanation or more documentation.

Condition

To consider **condition**, to answer the question about the financial condition of the applicant if the loan is made, the underwriter studies your credit report, using new numbers.

The lender's technician assumes that the loan has been made and puts in new numbers to see what your new financial condition would be. If you are refinancing and lowering your mortgage payments $300 a month, you should be in better condition after the loan. Conversely, a loan could make the applicant's position worse. Consider someone who has been renting an apartment for $500 a month and with the new loan would be making house payments of $1200.

The second set of assumptions requires much more study. First, income is compared with the new obligation. Second, savings are examined. If the applicant has solid income and savings or if the applicant would obviously have to struggle to make payments while assets and reserves would be depleted, decisions might be clear cut. When the answer is not so obvious, everything in the loan package is studied in the attempt to determine whether the applicant's financial condition will be acceptable.

From that study a picture emerges. If the picture is not clear, there may be a request for explanation or more documentation.

Questions about the Four Cs

One day you get a letter: "Congratulations. Your loan is conditionally approved." That sounds good, but do notice the word "conditionally." The more thoroughly the loan agent and the loan processor do their jobs, the fewer conditions there will be, but there always seems to be at least one condition. A list of common conditions-with notations of what must be done and who is responsible for seeing that the condition is removed –follows.

Condition	Reason/Resolution	Responsible Party
An easement or cloud appears on a title report.	Obtain clear title report.	Title company or attorney
Appraisal/comparable unacceptable or under valued.	Obtain current sold comparable support higher value.	Appraiser and/or Real estate agent
Termite or pest inspection needed.	Obtain clearance from pest inspector.	Real estate agent and/or Mortgage Broker
Credit report shows derogatory statements.	Obtain written letter of explanation and supporting documentation.	Applicant
Income verification not sufficient or out dated.	Obtain new pay stub or verification of employment.	Applicant and/or Lender/Broker

Amounts in bank accounts inconsistent with what is stated on application.	➤ Obtain current bank statements. Three months.	➤ Applicant
Proper vesting needed.	➤ Select best vesting.	➤ Applicant and/or Attorney
Inquiries appear on credit report.	➤ Obtain written letter of explanation.	➤ Applicant
Questions regarding allocation of loan proceeds.	➤ Written description and/or bids, plans, construction proposals.	➤ Applicant
Well/septic tank in question.	➤ Obtain clearance from inspector.	➤ Realtor and/or Lender/Broker
Flooring or misc. repair remarked as incomplete by appraiser.	➤ Obtain 442 certificate of completion.	➤ Appraiser
Loan requires mortgage insurance.	➤ Obtain insurance from MI company.	➤ Lender
AKA letter required.	➤ Also Known As - confirms same person.	➤ Applicant

100

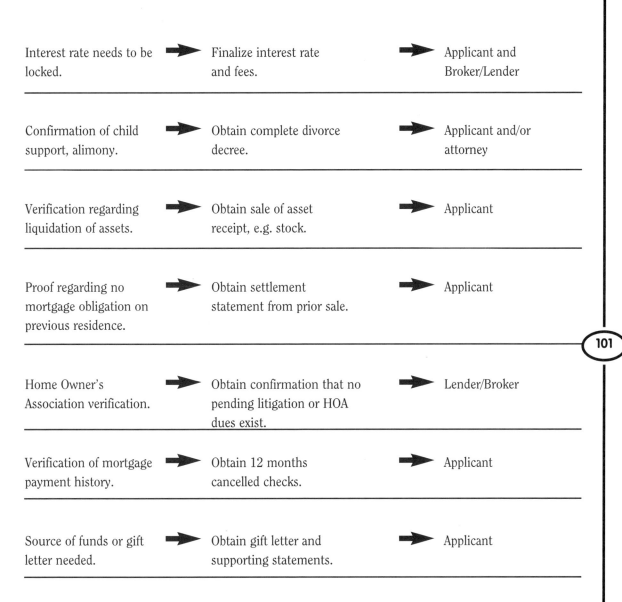

Interest rate needs to be locked. →	Finalize interest rate and fees. →	Applicant and Broker/Lender
Confirmation of child support, alimony. →	Obtain complete divorce decree. →	Applicant and/or attorney
Verification regarding liquidation of assets. →	Obtain sale of asset receipt, e.g. stock. →	Applicant
Proof regarding no mortgage obligation on previous residence. →	Obtain settlement statement from prior sale. →	Applicant
Home Owner's Association verification. →	Obtain confirmation that no pending litigation or HOA dues exist. →	Lender/Broker
Verification of mortgage payment history. →	Obtain 12 months cancelled checks. →	Applicant
Source of funds or gift letter needed. →	Obtain gift letter and supporting statements. →	Applicant

101

If by chance you cannot meet some condition, your approval may be revoked. If, for example, a condition for your approval is providing a pay stub showing $2,100 per month and because of downsizing your company reduces your salary to $1,900 per month, you can't meet that condition. If your new salary is not acceptable and no other solution is found, approval may be denied. You simply have to try somewhere else- or perhaps wait and try later.

#31 | HELPFUL HINT: Be annoyed if you want, but don't fight conditions. The lender has the right to ask for anything that could substantiate a decision. Besides, most conditions can be easily removed or satisfied.

102

CAUTION: A lender or broker might provide you with a letter stating that you have been approved for a loan of a certain amount. While such a letter may be useful in the sale of a property, it is a conditional approval. It should not be confused with a "letter to commit."

After the Four Cs

To this point, it seems that the decision is largely a matter of numbers: if the numbers are right, you get your loan; if they are not, you don't. But numbers can be read in more than one way. One lender may decline a loan and offer only one reason: the debt to income ratio is too high. The applicant protests that present monthly obligations are $3,000 and with the new loan would be under $2,700. Surely if the larger amount was being handled, the smaller amount would be. The same answer-too much debt to income-is repeated, and no other answer is given. (With a debt reduction loan, monthly payments for revolving accounts and installment loans might drop from $1,200 to $550 and still be turned down.) What such numbers may mean to that lender is that the applicant has shown a pattern of high debt and will simply incur more debt, continuing to owe more than is financially prudent, which makes default much more likely.

On the other hand, another lender may look at those same numbers and say that the applicant has had unfortunate experiences (divorce, illness, temporary unemployment) that caused the high debt and that the applicant is a good risk.

That is the subjective part of the decision. It may depend entirely on the lender and not on you. (That is why you must not assume that a **no** from one lender means **no** from all lenders.) You may not be able to influence that part of the decision directly, **but you can do something about the lender's impression of you.**

In fact, you can do something about the loan agent's impression of you.

Let us say very quickly:

> Creating a poor impression does not mean rejection.
> Creating a good impression does not mean approval.

Lenders and loan agents are in business. They want and expect to do business with any potential client. A carelessly prepared application, incomplete application, missing data or documents, ragged, torn, dirty, or poorly copied documents, conflicting information, tardy responses, and the like do not disqualify an applicant.

103

Conversely, a complete and carefully prepared application, a full set of documents that are easy to read and handle, complete and clear information, prompt responses, and the like do not mean that an application will be approved.

Let us add, however:

> Creating a good impression can help your cause.
> Creating a poor impression can hurt your cause.

The effect may be subconscious, but it is real. Thoughtfulness and attention can make your loan agent work better and harder, your lender more likely to say yes.

The Final Decision

After the lender has analyzed all the information, has looked at your loan package from all angles, a final decision can be made. If the decision is unfavorable, you will receive a written notice in the mail within three days. You can discuss with your loan agent the reasons for the decision and decide what to do.

If the decision is favorable, and our whole purpose here is to get a favorable response, you are almost through the maze. You are ready to take the final step.

Chapter Six

Out of the Maze:

Closing the Loan

You're at the end of the maze. As soon as you get past the paperwork, you can celebrate.

The closing of a loan is the time when last-minute wrinkles are ironed out, legal documents are reviewed, your loan is funded and recorded, and you sign your name, what seems to be, about 143 times.

You may have little or no contact with your lending agent during closing. The work of the lending agent is essentially finished. Your last action in getting the loan will be the signing of many documents. A closing agent, who will review with you all the documents you are signing, handles the signing session.

Your closing agent may be an attorney, a title officer, or an escrow officer; depending on which state the property is in. Some states use only attorneys, some only title or escrow officers; others use agents from two groups.

Earlier, we provided a list of conditions that you may have to meet. During closing, some condition everybody thought was removed always seems to pop up again. One more pay stub is needed. An explanatory letter concerning the co-borrower's other income is called for. An insurance premium you thought was covered is not covered and has to be paid with a cashier's check.

Expect the wrinkles and be pleased if they do not appear. It is possible for a loan to go through without wrinkles.

106

#31 HELPFUL HINT: If you are refinancing your home there may be some advantage to closing your loan at the end of the month rather than in the beginning or middle. Lenders call this time period "month end" and for most it's the last time of the month for them to get credit for a loan. It may mean very little to you but to lenders, it may mean more sales volume for the month and possible more commissions. During this time it is amazing how many conditions are "waved" in order to close the loan and meet quotas for that month.

Reviewing Legal Documents

Because each loan must meet its own requirements, any given loan may require other documents, but some of the most important legal documents should be mentioned here Descriptions and samples are provided on following pages.

Grant Deed

A Grant Deed conveys, or grants, title to a piece of property to the purchaser of that piece of property. The letters on the form indicate the points to note.

A. The official stamp, which confirms that your deed has been recorded
B. The name of the banking institution or private party which grants title to you
C. Your proper vesting
D. The legal description of your property (note that this address must be the same as is stated in your title report)
E. The officer of the lending institution or grantor of property
F. The official notary stamp and seal confirming that the signing of the document was witnessed

108

RECORDING REQUESTED BY

AND WHEN RECORDED MAIL THIS DEED AND, UNLESS
OTHERWISE SHOWN BELOW, MAIL TAX STATEMENTS TO:

NAME ⌐ Mr. C. Campbell

STREET
ADDRESS

CITY
STATE
ZIP ∟

574

```
RECORDED IN OFFICIAL RECORDS
OF LOS ANGELES COUNTY, CA.

SEP 29 1989    AT 8 A.M.

Recorder's Office
```
A

SURVEY MONUMENT FEE $10. CODE 9

FEE
$5
F

SPACE ABOVE THIS LINE FOR RECORDER'S USE

				ALL
				PTN

Title Order No.

Escrow or Loan No.

GRANT DEED

THE UNDERSIGNED GRANTOR(s) DECLARE(s)
DOCUMENTARY TRANSER TAX Is $ 363.00 _____ CITY TAX $ _____
☒ computed on full value of property conveyed, or
☐ computed on full value less value of liens or encumbrances remaining at time of sale,
☐ Unincorporated area: ☐ City of _____ , and

B

FOR A VALUABLE CONSIDERATION, receipt of which is hereby acknowledged,

(44)

C hereby GRANT(s) to
CEDRIC H. CAMPBELL

the following described real property in the   CITY AND

County of LOS ANGELES   State of California:

Parcel B of Parcel Map 42   as per map recorded in book   8 pages
 0 and 1 of Parcel Maps in the office of the county recorder of
said county.

D

apn: 2075

Dated September 27, 1989

E

STATE OF CALIFORNIA
COUNTY OF Los Angeles } SS
On September 27, 1989 before me, the
undersigned, a Notary Public in and for said State, personally appeared

_____ personally
known to me (or proved to me on the basis of satisfactory evidence) to
be the person___ whose name ___ subscribed to the within
instrument and acknowledged that ___ executed the same.
WITNESS my hand and official seal

Signature D.C. Kaplan

```
OFFICIAL SEAL
D. C. KAPLAN
NOTARY PUBLIC- CALIFORNIA
LOS ANGELES COUNTY
MY COMMISSION EXP. JULY 31, 1991
```
F

(This area for official notarial seal)

109

Deed of Trust

A Deed of Trust is a security instrument that conveys title to a particular piece of property in trust to a third party: a trustee, usually the bank that made the loan. The Deed is used to secure the payment of a note. The title is collateral security for the payment of a debt with the condition that the trustee shall reconvey the title upon the payment of the debt. The trustee has the power to sell the property and pay the debt in the event of a default by the debtor. In some states, the document used in place of a mortgage.

110

AFTER RECORDING
PLEASE MAIL TO:

MORTGAGE CORPORATION

LOAN NO. ——————————— [Space Above This Line For Recording Data] ————————————

DEED OF TRUST

THIS DEED OF TRUST ("Security Instrument") is made on ·   SEPTEMBER 28, 1993   The trustor is

("Borrower"). The trustee is

("Trustee"). The beneficiary is   MORTGAGE CORPORATION, A WISCONSIN CORPORATION

which is organized and existing under the laws of   THE STATE OF WISCONSIN   , and whose
address is
                                                            ("Lender"). Borrower owes Lender the principal sum of
  ONE HUNDRED TWENTY FIVE THOUSAND FIVE HUNDRED AND 00/100
                                              Dollars (U.S. $ 125500.00   ).
This debt is evidenced by Borrower's note dated the same date as this Security Instrument ("Note"), which provides for monthly
payments, with the full debt, if not paid earlier, due and payable on   OCTOBER 01, 2023   . This Security
Instrument secures to Lender: (a) the repayment of the debt evidenced by the Note, with interest, and all renewals, extensions and
modifications of the Note; (b) the payment of all other sums, with interest, advanced under paragraph 7 to protect the security of
this Security Instrument; and (c) the performance of Borrower's covenants and agreements under this Security Instrument and the
Note. For this purpose, Borrower irrevocably grants and conveys to Trustee, in trust, with power of sale, the following described
property located in   County, California:
  LEGAL DESCRIPTION IS ATTACHED HERETO AND MADE A PART HEREOF.

(111)

which has the address of   [Street, City],
California   93063   ("Property Address");
                   [Zip Code]
CALIFORNIA - Single Family - Fannie Mae/Freddie Mac UNIFORM INSTRUMENT   Page 1 of 6   Form 3005 9/90
VMP -6R(CA) (9101)   VMP MORTGAGE FORMS - (313)293-8100 - (800)521-7291   ✓   Initials: _____

Note or Security Instrument

A note is a written promise to pay a sum of money at a stated interest rate during a specified term. It is secured by a mortgage.

112

The first note shown is for a <u>Fixed Rate Mortgage</u>. Check the following items very carefully.

A..   Confirm that this is the amount you agreed to borrow
B.   Confirm that this is the interest rate you will be charged each year
C.   Recognize that even if you do not receive a payment reminder, you are obligated to
        make your monthly payments as promised to the institution specified
D.   Note that this is the agreed upon monthly payment for the next 30 years
E.   Understand the penalties for late payments
F.   Understand that this loan is not transferable or assumable by another borrower
        (If it is found that any such transfer has been made, the full balance may become
        immediately due and payable.)

NOTE   LOAN NO.

SEPTEMBER 28,, 1993   WEST HILLS   CALIFORNIA
                                      [City]   [State]

[Property Address]

1. BORROWER'S PROMISE TO PAY

In return for a loan that I have received, I promise to pay U.S. $ 125500.00 **A**   (this amount is called "principal"), plus interest, to the order of the Lender. The Lender is

MORTGAGE CORPORATION, A WISCONSIN CORPORATION   . I understand that the Lender may transfer this Note. The Lender or anyone who takes this Note by transfer and who is entitled to receive payments under this Note is called the "Note Holder".

2. INTEREST

Interest will be charged on unpaid principal until the full amount of principal has been paid. I will pay interest at a yearly **B** rate of   7.375   %.

The interest rate required by this Section 2 is the rate I will pay both before and after any default described in Section 6(B) of this Note.

3. PAYMENTS

(A) Time and Place of Payments

I will pay principal and interest by making payments every month.

I will make my monthly payments on the   1ST   day of each month beginning on   NOVEMBER 01, 19 93   . I will make these payments every month until I have paid all of the principal and interest and any other charges described below that I may owe under this Note. My monthly payments will be applied to interest before principal. If, on   OCTOBER 01,, 2023   , I still owe amounts under this Note, I will pay those amounts in full on that date, which is called the "Maturity Date".

I will make my monthly payments at   **C**   9275 NORTH 49TH STREET
                                             MILWAUKEE, WISCONSIN 53223
                                             or at a different place if required by the Note Holder.

(B) Amount of Monthly Payments

My monthly payment will be in the amount of U.S. $ 866.80 **D**

4. BORROWER'S RIGHT TO PREPAY

I have the right to make payments of principal at any time before they are due. A payment of principal only is known as a "prepayment". When I make a prepayment, I will tell the Note Holder in writing that I am doing so.

I may make a full prepayment or partial prepayments without paying any prepayment charge. The Note Holder will use all of my prepayments to reduce the amount of principal that I owe under this Note. If I make a partial prepayment, there will be no changes in the due date or in the amount of my monthly payment unless the Note Holder agrees in writing to those changes.

5. LOAN CHARGES

If a law, which applies to this loan and which sets maximum loan charges, is finally interpreted so that the interest or other loan charges collected or to be collected in connection with this loan exceed the permitted limits, then: (i) any such loan charge shall be reduced by the amount necessary to reduce the charge to the permitted limit; and (ii) any sums already collected from me which exceeded permitted limits will be refunded to me. The Note Holder may choose to make this refund by reducing the principal I owe under this Note or by making a direct payment to me. If a refund reduces principal, the reduction will be treated as a partial prepayment.

6. BORROWER'S FAILURE TO PAY AS REQUIRED

(A) Late Charge for Overdue Payments   **E**

If the Note Holder has not received the full amount of any monthly payment by the end of   FIFTEEN   calendar days after the date it is due, I will pay a late charge to the Note Holder. The amount of the charge will be   5.00   % of my overdue payment of principal and interest. I will pay this late charge promptly but only once on each late payment.

(B) Default

If I do not pay the full amount of each monthly payment on the date it is due, I will be in default.

(C) Notice of Default

If I am in default, the Note Holder may send me a written notice telling me that if I do not pay the overdue amount by a certain date, the Note Holder may require me to pay immediately the full amount of principal which has not been paid and all the interest that I owe on that amount. That date must be at least 30 days after the date on which the notice is delivered or mailed to me.

(D) No Waiver By Note Holder

Even if, at a time when I am in default, the Note Holder does not require me to pay immediately in full as described above, the Note Holder will still have the right to do so if I am in default at a later time.

(E) Payment of Note Holder's Costs and Expenses

If the Note Holder has required me to pay immediately in full as described above, the Note Holder will have the right to be paid back by me for all of its costs and expenses in enforcing this Note to the extent not prohibited by applicable law. Those expenses include, for example, reasonable attorneys' fees.

7. GIVING OF NOTICES

Unless applicable law requires a different method, any notice that must be given to me under this Note will be given by delivering it or by mailing it by first class mail to me at the Property Address above or at a different address if I give the Note Holder a notice of my different address.

Any notice that must be given to the Note Holder under this Note will be given by mailing it by first class mail to the Note Holder at the address stated in Section 3(A) above or at a different address if I am given a notice of that different address.

9. OBLIGATIONS OF PERSONS UNDER THIS NOTE

If more than one person signs this Note, each person is fully and personally obligated to keep all of the promises made in this Note, including the promise to pay the full amount owed. Any person who is a guarantor, surety or endorser of this Note is also obligated to do these things. Any person who takes over these obligations, including the obligations of a guarantor, surety or endorser of this Note, is also obligated to keep all of the promises made in this Note. The Note Holder may enforce its rights under this Note against each person individually or against all of us together. This means that any one of us may be required to pay all of the amounts owed under this Note.

10. WAIVERS

I and any other person who has obligations under this Note waive the rights of presentment and notice of dishonor. "Presentment" means the right to require the Note Holder to demand payment of amounts due. "Notice of dishonor" means the right to require the Note Holder to give notice to other persons that amounts due have not been paid.

11. UNIFORM SECURED NOTE

This Note is a uniform instrument with limited variations in some jurisdictions. In addition to the protections given to the Note Holder under this Note, a Mortgage, Deed of Trust or Security Deed (the "Security Instrument"), dated the same date as this Note, protects the Note Holder from possible losses which might result if I do not keep the promises that I make in this Note. That Security Instrument describes how and under what conditions I may be required to make immediate payment in full of all amounts I owe under this Note. Some of those conditions are described as follows:

Transfer of the Property or a Beneficial Interest in Borrower. If all or any part of the Property or any interest in it is sold or transferred (or if a beneficial interest in Borrower is sold or transferred and Borrower is not a natural person) without Lender's prior written consent, Lender may, at its option, require immediate payment in full of all sums secured by this Security Instrument. However, this option shall not be exercised by Lender if exercise is prohibited by federal law as of the date of this Security Instrument. Lender also shall not exercise this option if: (a) Borrower causes to be submitted to Lender information required by Lender to evaluate the intended transferee as if a new loan were being made to the transferee; and (b) Lender reasonably determines that Lender's security will not be impaired by the loan assumption and that the risk of a breach of any covenant or agreement in this Security Instrument is acceptable to Lender.

To the extent permitted by applicable law, Lender may charge a reasonable fee as a condition to Lender's consent to the loan assumption. Lender may also require the transferee to sign an assumption agreement that is acceptable to Lender and that obligates the transferee to keep all the promises and agreements made in the Note and in this Security Instrument. Borrower will continue to be obligated under the Note and this Security Instrument unless Lender releases Borrower in writing.

If Lender exercises the option to require immediate payment in full, Lender shall give Borrower notice of acceleration. The notice shall provide a period of not less than 30 days from the date the notice is delivered or mailed within which Borrower must pay all sums secured by this Security Instrument. If Borrower fails to pay these sums prior to the expiration of this period, Lender may invoke any remedies permitted by this Security Instrument without further notice or demand on Borrower.

WITNESS THE HAND(S) AND SEAL(S) OF THE UNDERSIGNED.

. . . .(Seal)
-Borrower

. . . .(Seal)
-Borrower

. . . .(Seal)
-Borrower

[Sign Original Only]

Notes...

Adjustable Rate Mortgage

The next note shown is for an <u>Adjustable Rate Mortgage</u>. Most of the items on an ARM note are the same an FRM. There are, however, differences to be noted.

A.   The ARM note includes a periodic rate change date. (The interest rate on the note shown changes every 6 months and is therefore termed a 6 month ARM.)

B.   The ARM note indicates the index used to set rates. (The index in the note shown is the LIBOR.)

C.   The ARM note includes a clause that shows what the margin is and how it is used to calculate future payments.

D.   The ARM note confirms the periodic and lifetime caps on the loan. (The note shown starts at a 5% rate with a 1% periodic cap up or down, which means the rate could move to 4% or 6%. The 6% lifetime cap limits the maximum interest rate to 11 %.)

E.   The ARM note, unlike the FRM note, allows assumability and explains the way it works.

ADJUSTABLE RATE NOTE
(LIBOR Index-Rate Caps)

THIS NOTE CONTAINS PROVISIONS ALLOWING FOR CHANGES IN MY INTEREST RATE AND MY MONTHLY PAYMENT. THIS NOTE LIMITS THE AMOUNT MY INTEREST RATE CAN CHANGE AT ANY ONE TIME AND THE MAXIMUM RATE I MUST PAY.

September 29th . . . . . , 19 93 . .   Westlake Village . . . . . . ,   California . . . .
                                              [City]   [State]

. . . . [Property Address] . . . .

1. BORROWER'S PROMISE TO PAY

In return for a loan that I have received, I promise to pay U.S. $ . . . . . 118,000.00 (this amount is called "principal"), plus interest, to the order of the Lender. The Lender is . . . .
. . . . FINANCIAL CORPORATION . . . .
I understand that the Lender may transfer this Note. The Lender or anyone who takes this Note by transfer and who is entitled to receive payments under this Note is called the "Note Holder."

2. INTEREST

Interest will be charged on unpaid principal until the full amount of principal has been paid. I will pay interest at a yearly rate of . . . . 5.000 . . %. The interest rate I will pay may change in accordance with Section 4 of this Note.

The interest rate required by this Section 2 and Section 4 of this Note is the rate I will pay both before and after any default described in Section 7(B) of this Note.

3. PAYMENTS

(A) Time and Place of Payments

I will pay principal and interest by making payments every month.

I will make my monthly payments on the first day of each month beginning on . December First . . . . 19 93 . . . . I will make these payments every month until I have paid all of the principal and interest and any other charges described below that I may owe under this Note. My monthly payments will be applied to interest before principal. If, on November 1st, 2023 . . . . , I still owe amounts under this Note, I will pay those amounts in full on that date, which is called the "maturity date."

I will make my monthly payments at . . . North . . . . Street . . . .
. . . . CA, ... or at a different place if required by the Note Holder.

(B) Amount of My Initial Monthly Payments

Each of my initial monthly payments will be in the amount of U.S. $ . . 633.45 . . . . . This amount may change.

(C) Monthly Payment Changes

Changes in my monthly payment will reflect changes in the unpaid principal of my loan and in the interest rate that I must pay. The Note Holder will determine my new interest rate and the changed amount of my monthly payment in accordance with Section 4 of this Note.

4. INTEREST RATE AND MONTHLY PAYMENT CHANGES

(A) Change Dates

A

The interest rate I will pay may change on the first day of . . May . . . . . , 19 . . . 94 . . . , and on that day every sixth month thereafter. Each date on which my interest rate could change is called a "Change Date."

(B) The Index **B**

Beginning with the first Change Date, my interest rate will be based on an Index. The "Index" is the average on interbank offered rates for six-month U.S. dollar-denominated deposits in the London market ("LIBOR"), as published in *The Wall Street Journal*. The most recent Index figure available as of the first business day of the month immediately preceding the month in which the Change Date occurs is called the "Current Index."

If the Index is no longer available, the Note Holder will choose a new index that is based upon comparable information. The Note Holder will give me notice of this choice.

(C) Calculation of Changes

C

Before each Change Date, the Note Holder will calculate my new interest rate by adding . Two and Five-Eighths . . . . percentage points (. . 2.625 %) to the Current Index. The Note Holder will then round the result of this addition to the nearest one-eighth of one percentage point (0.125%). Subject to the limits stated in Section 4(D) below, this rounded amount will be my new interest rate until the next Change Date.

117

The Note Holder will then determine the amount of the monthly payment that would be sufficient to repay the unpaid principal that I am expected to owe at the Change Date in full on the maturity date at my new interest rate in substantially equal payments. The result of this calculation will be the new amount of my monthly payment.

(D) Limits on Interest Rate Changes **D**

The interest rate I am required to pay at the first Change Date will not be greater than 6.000 % or less than 4.000 %. Thereafter, my interest rate will never be increased or decreased on any single Change Date by more than one percentage point (1%) from the rate of interest I have been paying for the preceding six months. My interest rate will never be greater than 11.000 %.

(E) Effective Date of Changes

My new interest rate will become effective on each Change Date. I will pay the amount of my new monthly payment beginning on the first monthly payment date after the Change Date until the amount of my monthly payment changes again.

(F) Notice of Changes

The Note Holder will deliver or mail to me a notice of any changes in my interest rate and the amount of my monthly payment before the effective date of any change. The notice will include information required by law to be given me and also the title and telephone number of a person who will answer any question I may have regarding the notice.

5.   BORROWER'S RIGHT TO PREPAY

I have the right to make payments of principal at any time before they are due. A payment of principal only is known as a "prepayment." When I make a prepayment, I will tell the Note Holder in writing that I am doing so.

I may make a full prepayment or partial prepayments without paying any prepayment charge. The Note Holder will use all of my prepayments to reduce the amount of principal that I owe under this Note. If I make a partial prepayment, there will be no changes in the due dates of my monthly payments unless the Note Holder agrees in writing to those changes. My partial prepayment may reduce the amount of my monthly payments after the first Change Date following my partial prepayment. However, any reduction due to my partial prepayment may be offset by an interest rate increase.

6. LOAN CHARGES

If a law, which applies to this loan and which sets maximum loan charges, is finally interpreted so that the interest or other loan charges collected or to be collected in connection with this loan exceed the permitted limits, then: (i) any such loan charge shall be reduced by the amount necessary to reduce the charge to the permitted limit; and (ii) any sums already collected from me which exceeded permitted limits will be refunded to me. The Note Holder may choose to make this refund by reducing the principal I owe under this Note or by making a direct payment to me. If a refund reduces principal, the reduction will be treated as a partial prepayment.

7. BORROWER'S FAILURE TO PAY AS REQUIRED

(A) Late Charges for Overdue Payments

If the Note Holder has not received the full amount of any monthly payment by the end of 15 calendar days after the date it is due, I will pay a late charge to the Note Holder. The amount of the charge will be 5.0 % of my overdue payment of principal and interest. I will pay this late charge promptly but only once on each late payment.

(B) Default

If I do not pay the full amount of each monthly payment on the date it is due, I will be in default.

(C) Notice of Default

If I am in default, the Note Holder may send me a written notice telling me that if I do not pay the overdue amount by a certain date, the Note Holder may require me to pay immediately the full amount of principal which has not been paid and all the interest that I owe on that amount. That date must be at least 30 days after the date on which the notice is delivered or mailed to me.

(D) No Waiver By Note Holder

Even if, at a time when I am in default, the Note Holder does not require me to pay immediately in full as described above, the Note Holder will still have the right to do so if I am in default at a later time.

(E) Payment of Note Holder's Costs and Expenses

If the Note Holder has required me to pay immediately in full as described above, the Note Holder will have the right to be paid back by me for all of its costs and expenses in enforcing this Note to the extent not prohibited by applicable law. Those expenses include, for example, reasonable attorneys' fees.

8.   GIVING OF NOTICES

Unless applicable law requires a different method, any notice that must be given to me under this Note will be given by delivering it or by mailing it by first class mail to me at the Property Address above or at a different address if I give the Note Holder a notice of my different address.

Any notice that must be given to the Note Holder under this Note will be given by mailing it by first class mail to the Note Holder at the address stated in Section 3(A) above or at a different address if I am given a notice of that different address.

LOAN NO.

8. OBLIGATIONS OF PERSONS UNDER THIS NOTE

If more than one person signs this Note, each person is fully and personally obligated to keep all of the promises made in this Note, including the promise to pay the full amount owed. Any person who is a guarantor, surety or endorser of this Note is also obligated to do these things. Any person who takes over these obligations, including the obligations of a guarantor, surety or endorser of this Note, is also obligated to keep all of the promises made in this Note. The Note Holder may enforce its rights under this Note against each person individually or against all of us together. This means that any one of us may be required to pay all of the amounts owed under this Note.

9. WAIVERS

I and any other person who has obligations under this Note waive the rights of presentment and notice of dishonor. "Presentment" means the right to require the Note Holder to demand payment of amounts due. "Notice of dishonor" means the right to require the Note Holder to give notice to other persons that amounts due have not been paid.

10. UNIFORM SECURED NOTE

This Note is a uniform instrument with limited variations in some jurisdictions. In addition to the protections given to the Note Holder under this Note, a Mortgage, Deed of Trust or Security Deed (the "Security Instrument"), dated the same date as this Note, protects the Note Holder from possible losses which might result if I do not keep the promises which I make in this Note. That Security Instrument describes how and under what conditions I may be required to make immediate payment in full of all amounts I owe under this Note. Some of those conditions are described as follows:

F   Transfer of the Property or a Beneficial Interest in Borrower. If all or any part of the Property or any interest in it is sold or transferred (or if a beneficial interest in Borrower is sold or transferred and Borrower is not a natural person) without Lender's prior written consent, Lender may, at its option, require immediate payment in full of all sums secured by this Security Instrument. However, this option shall not be exercised by Lender if exercise is prohibited by federal law as of the date of this Security Instrument.

If Lender exercises this option, Lender shall give Borrower notice of acceleration. The notice shall provide a period of not less than 30 days from the date the notice is delivered or mailed within which Borrower must pay all sums secured by this Security Instrument. If Borrower fails to pay these sums prior to the expiration of this period, Lender may invoke any remedies permitted by this Security Instrument without further notice or demand on Borrower.

119

WITNESS THE HAND(S) AND SEAL(S) OF THE UNDERSIGNED.

_____(Seal)
-Borrower

___(Seal)
-Borrower

_____(Seal).
-Borrower

_____(Seal)
-Borrower
(Sign Original Only)

Settlement Statement/HUD 1

The written document outlines money paid by borrowers and sellers to effect the closing of a mortgage loan. Items paid normally include an origination fee, discount points, title insurance, survey, attorney or escrow fee, such prepaid items as taxes and insurance, and escrow payments. The statement is the final breakdown of closing costs and distribution of loan proceeds. The total should match your GFE within $500. The following items should be noted.

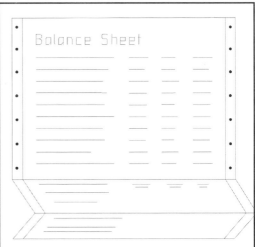

a.   Cost of the loan (broken down further on the second page)

b.   Amount of the loan

c.   Proceeds from the loan (statement suggests that borrower will receive approximately $ 10,000 in cash)

d.   Details of loan cost (borrower charged 1.625% points and other listed charges)

e.   Prepaid interest (always collected on a new loan-usually, 30 days' interest with any amount not needed refunded after the loan closes)

If you are refinancing a loan, there is a good chance you will receive unused interest when your old loan is paid. If, for example, you make a payment on the old loan on the first of the month and that loan is paid off on the 15th, you will be entitled to reimbursement of 15 days' interest on your old loan and 15 days on your new loan.

#33 | HELPFUL HINT: Many lenders will increase your loan amount to cover all expenses so that you will not be inconvenienced by having to pay extra money to escrow to close your loan. Because prepaid interest is considered an expense, the lender will raise your loan to cover expenses. Considering that these are monies you will probably be refunded shortly, it would be to your advantage, if possible, to pay those as out of pocket expenses. That way you won't pay points on that money or increase your payments over the long run.

f. Closing agent or escrow fee
g. Title insurance policy fee
h. Payoff of existing loan

Please note that your loan balance is not-as it might seem-$120,000 based on banking/mortgage statements. It is not uncommon that when a "demand" statement requests the amount required to pay off an existing loan, the current lender may include servicing fees, administration fees, past late fees, interest, etc. The net result is that although the balance may be $120,000, the demand balance may be $122,000.

OMB No. 2502-0265

A. U.S. DEPARTMENT OF HOUSING AND URBAN DEVELOPMENT SETTLEMENT STATEMENT	B.	B. TYPE OF LOAN

B. TYPE OF LOAN

1. ☐ FHA   2. ☐ FMHA   3. ☐ CONV. UNINS.

4. ☐ VA   5. ☐ CONV. INS.

6. FILE NUMBER	7. LOAN NUMBER

8. MORTGAGE INSURANCE CASE NUMBER

C. NOTE: This form is furnished to give you a statement of actual settlement costs. Amounts paid to and by the settlement agent are shown. Items marked "(P.O.C.)" were paid outside the closing; they are shown here for informational purposes and are not included in the totals.

D. NAME OF BORROWER	E. NAME OF SELLER
F. NAME OF LENDER	G. PROPERTY LOCATION

H. SETTLEMENT AGENT	PLACE OF SETTLEMENT	I. SETTLEMENT DATE
ESCROW, INC.	South Westlake Boulevard Westlake Village CA 91361	Nov. 18, 1992

J. SUMMARY OF BORROWER'S TRANSACTION:		K. SUMMARY OF SELLER'S TRANSACTION:	
100. GROSS AMOUNT DUE FROM BORROWER		400. GROSS AMOUNT DUE TO SELLER	
101. Contract sales price		401. Contract sales price	
102. Personal property **A**		402. Personal property	
103. Settlement charges to borrower (line 1400)	4,961.16	403.	
104. See Attached for Breakdown	123,589.99	404.	
105. Tax Payment	1,153.35	405.	
Adjustments for items paid by seller in advance		Adjustments for items paid by seller in advance	
106. City/town taxes to		406. City/town taxes to	
107. County taxes to		407. County taxes to	
108. Assessments to		408. Assessments to	
109.		409.	
110.		410.	
120. GROSS AMOUNT DUE FROM BORROWER	129,704.50	420. GROSS AMOUNT DUE TO SELLER	
200. AMOUNTS PAID BY OR ON BEHALF OF BORROWER		500. REDUCTIONS IN AMOUNT DUE TO SELLER	
201. Deposit or earnest money		501. Excess deposit (see instructions)	
202. Principal amount of new loan(s) **B**	140,000.00	502. Settlement charges to seller (line 1400)	
203. Existing loan(s) taken subject to		503. Existing loan(s) taken subject to	
204. Second mortgage loan		504. Payoff of first mortgage loan	
		Principal Balance $	
		Interest Adjustment $	
		Reserves ( ) Credit ( ) Deficit $	
205.		505. Payoff of second mortgage loan	
		Principal Balance $	
		Interest Adjustment $	
206.		506. Second mortgage loan to borrower	
207.		507.	
208.		508.	
209.			
Adjustments for items unpaid by seller		Adjustments for items unpaid by seller	
210. City/town taxes to		510. City/town taxes to	
211. County taxes to		511. County taxes to	
212. Assessments to		512. Assessments to	
213.		513.	
214.		514.	
215.		515.	
216.		516.	
217.		517.	
220. TOTAL PAID BY/FOR BORROWER	140,000.00	520. TOTAL REDUCTION AMOUNT DUE SELLER	
300. CASH AT SETTLEMENT FROM OR TO BORROWER		600. CASH AT SETTLEMENT TO OR FROM SELLER	
301. Gross amount due from borrower (line 120)	129,704.50	601. Gross amount due to seller (line 420)	
302. Less amounts paid by/for borrower (line 220)	(140,000.00)	602. Less reduction amount due seller (line 520)	( )
303. CASH (☐FROM) ☒(☐TO) BORROWER **C**	10,295.50	603. CASH (☐TO) (☐FROM) SELLER	

CERTIFIED TO BE A TRUE AND EXACT COPY OF THE ORIGINAL.

BY:

CO-442-1 (3-90)

HUD-1
RESPA, HB 4305.2

122

U.S. DEPARTMENT OF HOUSING AND URBAN DEVELOPMENT
SETTLEMENT STATEMENT
PAGE 2

L. SETTLEMENT CHARGES			PAID FROM BORROWER'S FUNDS AT SETTLEMENT	PAID FROM SELLER'S FUNDS AT SETTLEMENT
700.	TOTAL SALES/BROKER'S COMMISSION based on price $ @ % =			
	Division of Commission (line 700) as follows:			
701.	$ to			
702.	$ to			
703.	Commission paid at settlement			
704.				
800.	ITEMS PAYABLE IN CONNECTION WITH LOAN D			
801.	Loan Origination Fee 1.6250 %		2,275.00	
802.	Loan Discount %			
803.	Appraisal Fee to REVIEW		150.00	
804.	Credit Report to			
805.	Lender's Inspection Fee			
806.	Mortgage Insurance Application Fee to			
807.	Assumption Fee			
808.	Tax Service Contract		98.00	
809.	DOC PREP FEE		150.00	
810.	ADMINISTRATION FEE		395.00	
811.	WIRE FEE		35.00	
812.				
813.				
900.	ITEMS REQUIRED BY LENDER TO BE PAID IN ADVANCE			
901.	Interest from 11/17/92 to 12/01/92 @ $ 30.14000 E /day		421.96	
902.	Mortgage Insurance Premium for mo. to			
903.	Hazard Insurance Premium for 1 yrs. to INSURANCE		409.00	
904.	Flood Insurance Premium for yrs. to			
905.				
1000.	RESERVES DEPOSITED WITH LENDER FOR			
1001.	Hazard Insurance mo. @ $ per month			
1002.	Mortgage Insurance mo. @ $ per month			
1003.	City Property Taxes mo. @ $ per month			
1004.	County Property Taxes mo. @ $ per month			
1005.	Annual Assessments mo. @ $ per month			
1006.	Flood Insurance mo. @ $ per month			
1007.	mo. @ $ per month			
1008.	mo. @ $ per month			
1100.	TITLE CHARGES			
1101.	Settlement or Closing Fee to ESCROW, INC. F		349.00	
1102.	Abstract or Title Search to			
1103.	Title Examination to			
1104.	Title Insurance Binder to			
1105.	Document Preparation to			
1106.	Notary Fees to		20.00	
1107.	Attorney's Fees to			
	(includes above items No.:)			
1108.	Title Insurance to TITLE CO. G		494.20	
	(includes above items No.:)			
1109.	Lender's coverage $ 140,000.00			
1110.	Owner's coverage $			
1111.				
1112.	See Attached for Breakdown		125.00	
1113.				
1200.	GOVERNMENT RECORDING AND TRANSFER CHARGES			
1201.	Recording Fees: Deed $; Mortgage $ 23.00 ; Release $ 16.00		39.00	
1202.	City/County Tax/Stamps: Deed $; Mortgage $			
1203.	State Tax/Stamps: Deed $; Mortgage $			
1204.				
1205.				
1300.	ADDITIONAL SETTLEMENT CHARGES			
1301.	Survey to			
1302.	Pest Inspection to			
1303.				
1304.				
1305.				
1400.	TOTAL SETTLEMENT CHARGES (enter on lines 103, Section J and 502, Section K)		4,961.16	

CO-442-2 (3-90)

123

HUD-1

CERTIFIED TO BE A TRUE
AND EXACT COPY OF THE
ORIGINAL
BY:

HUD SETTLEMENT STATEMENT BREAKDOWN FOR ESCROW

DATE : Nov. 18, 1992   PAGE : 3
                              BORROWER

PROPERTY   :

BORROWER(S):

SELLER(S) :

HUD LINE #	DESCRIPTION		AMOUNT
104	Existing 1st Principal Balance	H	122,981.04
	Interest		608.95
	TOTAL HUD 104		$123,589.99
1112	FEDERAL EXPRESS		15.00
	Title Company Sub-Escrow Fee		35.00
	Reconveyance Fee		75.00
	TOTAL HUD 1112		$125.00

124

Notes...

<u>Notice to Rescind</u>

A Notice to Rescind is a statement of cancellation or annulment of a transaction or contract by the operation of law or by mutual consent. By law a borrower is allowed three full days to review details of a mortgage and cancel if it decided that obtaining the loan is not prudent. Borrowers can get caught up in the idea of refinancing a house to get cash to start a business and qualify for a loan that would become a great burden. The three days of reflection might preclude a big mistake.

Rescission are offered on all loans involving equity with the exception of new home purchases and refinances of rental or investment properties.

Note that the right exists-except as just indicated-and note two dates.

A. the date the loan was signed
B. the last date it is possible to rescind that loan

Those days should be calculated in your time frames if you need funds by a certain date.

NOTICE OF RIGHT TO CANCEL

Transaction I.D. No.   Loan Number
Borrowers:

Property Address:

YOUR RIGHT TO CANCEL:

You are entering into a transaction that will result in a mortgage, lien, or security interest on/in your home. You have a legal right under federal law to cancel this transaction, without cost, within three business days from whichever of the following events occurs last:

1. the date of the transaction, which is   ; or *10 - 4 - 93* **A**
2. the date you receive your Truth in Lending disclosures; or
3. the date you receive this notice of your right to cancel.

If you cancel the transaction, the mortgage, lien, or security interest is also cancelled. Within 20 calendar days after we receive your notice, we must take the steps necessary to reflect the fact that the mortgage, lien, or security interest on/in your home has been cancelled, and we must return to you any money or property you have given to us or to anyone else in connection with this transaction.

You may keep any money or property we have given you until we have done the things mentioned above, but you must then offer to return the money or property. If it is impractical or unfair for you to return the property, you must offer its reasonable value. You may offer to return the property at your home or at the location of the property. Money must be returned to the address below. If we do not take possession of the money or property within 20 calendar days of your offer, you may keep it without further obligation.

HOW TO CANCEL:

If you decide to cancel this transaction, you may do so by notifying us in writing,

Name of Creditor

at

You may use any written statement that is signed and dated by you and states your intention to cancel, or you may use this notice by dating and signing below. Keep one copy of this notice because it contains important information about your rights.

If you cancel by mail or telegram, you must send a notice no later than midnight of *10/7/93* **B** (or midnight of the third business day following the latest of the three events listed above.) If you send or deliver your written notice to cancel some other way, it must be delivered to the above address no later than that time.

I WISH TO CANCEL

_____   _____
Date   Consumer's Signature

ON THE DATE LISTED ABOVE I/WE UNDERSIGNED EACH RECEIVED TWO (2) COMPLETED COPIES OF THE NOTICE OF RIGHT TO CANCEL IN THE FORM PRESCRIBED BY LAW ADVISING ME/US OF MY/OUR RIGHT TO CANCEL THIS TRANSACTION.

127

<u>Recording the Loan</u>

Once your loan has funded, that is, monies have been transferred to the lender from a given funding source, your loan will be recorded in the county registrar's office. The recording includes the details of a properly executed legal document such as a deed, mortgage, satisfaction of mortgage during a refinance, or an extension of mortgage, thereby making it part of public record. In some counties, recording can be done the same day the loan is funded. If not, it is generally done the next business day. The day is important to know because there may be some liability if you allow someone to move into a house before a sale is recorded.

<u>Signing the Papers</u>

When all the papers have been processed, you and the escrow officer, title officer, or attorney of record will sit down, and you'll be handed one document after another and told to sign here, here, and here and initial there and there. If two or three of you are signing, you'll pass the documents from one to another, each being careful to leave room for other signatures or initials. The officer will explain what you're signing. If your loan agent has been thorough, you'll be prepared for the content and purpose of what you're signing. If your loan agent has not told you all you need to know you'll be hearing some things you don't want to hear for the first time.

#34 | HELPFUL HINT: Obtaining a copy of your estimated settlement statement from your closing agent before you sign your loan documents could save you time and money. You may find some inconsistencies in interest rate, costs, or other agreements you made with your lender or broker. Your loan closing should not be a surprise party. You should be able to walk in, review your documents, and understand and agree with all your fees.

It is now common practice for your signing to be notarized, and many states require finger printing, both of which are done at the time of closing. You will need photo identification at that time, but nothing else is required of you.

Living with Your Loan

When you finish signing, you've made it. You're through the maze.

First, you relax. Then you give and receive congratulations. Celebrate if you want.

Because you pay some interest through the closing process and because you'll be paying for the month before instead of the month ahead (even though payments are due on the first of the month), you will have a month, maybe two, before you make a payment. During that time, your loan may be sold to a "loan servicer," a company that handles your monthly billings and tax impounds if required. It is very possible that your loan will be sold several times during its life, sometimes without your even knowing. If your loan is with a bank or a savings bank, you'll receive a monthly statement showing what is due, when it's due, how much interest you've paid, and what your current balance is. If you go to a lender through a broker, you may be mailed a book of coupons, one for each month.

It is your responsibility to make payments without reminders. Even if you don't receive a statement or a coupon book, you have obligated yourself to make payments as indicated in the closing instructions. Do make those payments. Late payments work against you. Remember FICO scores?

That a mortgage may be sold two or three times in the first two months makes no difference to the borrower in the terms of the loan (even though it may make some borrowers nervous). Your payment structure should not change. Except for mechanical matters such as statements, coupons, and mailing devices, everything should remain the same.

#35

> HELPFUL HINT: If you receive notice of a change in mortgage holders from both companies, simply follow the instructions for making payments, but if you get a notice from only the new company, you'd better check with the original company before sending money to the new company. Servicing fraud is a big business, and you could lose more than just your monthly payment.

131

You can live with your loan very nicely: Just keep up the payments, think about the advantages of home ownership, and enjoy your home.

Summary

That concludes your trip through the mortgage maze. Don't be concerned if you're still not clear about the entire route and all the steps. Few people are fully clear-not even all the people in the business. Besides, as has been noted in several places, each loan is different. We're not simply memorizing the route through one maze; we're learning to read the map for any maze because you may journey through the mortgage maze many times yourself or on behalf of someone else.

First, the mortgage business itself constantly changes-not just interest and points but rules, regulations, and practices-and the professional must be current on everything. Second, things change in the life of the borrower (change of job, larger or smaller family, different debt structure, a room addition), which means that the loan application made two years ago to buy a house wouldn't work for refinancing the house today-even if nothing changed in the business. Third, the combination of business changes and personal changes means more concern about being current.

What doesn't change is the necessity to be informed and aware as you go in, to be prepared. That is what I've kept in mind while working on this guidebook; it should help you get through the mortgage maze with much more confidence and efficiency and with fewer upsets and surprises. You won't have to suffer that dreaded feeling of being at the mercy of someone else.

The role you play in the loan process is as big as you make it. The loan agent won't mind at all if you gather more information, check more facts, and make more decisions. All the information that is used to decide whether you get a loan comes from you. The earlier and the more thoroughly you get all relevant information-the favorable and the unfavorable-to your loan agent, the more the loan agent can do for you. The worst thing you can do is to reveal something critical four weeks into the process. Your loan agent needs your openness and honesty. Knowing about negative matters, the loan agent can do something about them. What your loan agent doesn't know, the lender will learn, and that raises a red flag about you and everything in your file.

You've been told that few (if any) loans go through without problems. There are too many people handling too many pieces of paper not to have some surprises, some snags. But you've also been told that you can deal with those problems. An appraisal that is a bit low or a cloud on the title need not be a cause for agitation, anger, or anxiety.

> **Millions of other borrowers have handled those events, and so can you.**

Without trying to compare a mortgage to a baby, we could say that when the new baby arrives, the proud parents forget that the baby was two weeks late, that the mother had back pains and morning sickness, and that the father couldn't sleep for the last three months. Similarly, when the loan closes, you'll forget the time you spent gathering papers, the frustration of not knowing, and the feeling that your privacy has been invaded.

In the preface, I expressed my personal and professional commitment to do what I can to assure that clients (as well as loan agents) are well-informed. Let me reaffirm that commitment. The process of getting a mortgage can be exciting, but even if it is not exciting, at least it should be without pain. The results of that process should provide satisfaction the day of closing and for years to come.

If this guidebook helps you through the mortgage maze, I'd be pleased to know it. If you have a problem because something isn't clear or something you wanted to know isn't covered, I need to know that. I would appreciate a letter through my publisher, Frederick Fell Publishers Inc.

Appendix A

Mortgage/Loan Payment Comparison Table

Payments Made Monthly

Mortgage/Loan Payment Comparison Table - Payments Made Monthly

Interest Rates	Principal Amounts Amortized Over 30 Years				
	$70,000.00	$75,000.00	$80,000.00	$85,000.00	$90,000.00
4.0%	$334.20	$358.07	$381.94	$405.81	$429.68
4.5%	$354.68	$380.02	$405.35	$430.69	$456.02
5.0%	$375.78	$402.62	$429.46	$456.30	$483.14
5.5%	$397.46	$425.85	$454.24	$482.63	$511.02
6.0%	$419.69	$449.67	$479.65	$509.62	$539.60
6.5%	$442.45	$474.06	$505.66	$537.26	$568.87
7.0%	$465.72	$498.98	$532.25	$565.51	$598.78
7.5%	$489.46	$524.42	$559.38	$594.34	$629.30
8.0%	$513.64	$550.33	$587.02	$623.70	$660.39
8.5%	$538.24	$576.69	$615.14	$653.58	$692.03
9.0%	$563.24	$603.47	$643.70	$683.93	$724.17
9.5%	$588.60	$630.65	$672.69	$714.73	$756.77
10.0%	$614.31	$658.18	$702.06	$745.94	$789.82
10.5%	$640.32	$686.06	$731.80	$777.53	$823.27
11.0%	$666.63	$714.25	$761.86	$809.48	$857.10

Interest Rates	Principal Amounts Amortized Over 30 Years				
	$95,000.00	$100,000.00	$105,060.00	$110,000.00	$115,000.00
4.0%	$453.55	$477.42	$501.29	$525.16	$549.03
4.5%	$481.36	$506.69	$532.02	$557.36	$582.69
5.0%	$509.99	$536.83	$563.67	$590.51	$617.35
5.5%	$539.40	$567.79	$596.18	$624.57	$652.96
6.0%	$569.58	$599.56	$629.53	$659.51	$689.49
6.5%	$600.47	$632.07	$663.68	$695.28	$726.88
7.0%	$632.04	$665.31	$699.57	$731.84	$765.10
7.5%	$664.26	$699.22	$734.18	$769.14	$804.10
8.0%	$697.08	$733.77	$770.46	$807.15	$843.83
8.5%	$730.47	$768.92	$807.36	$845.81	$884.26
9.0%	$764.40	$804.63	$844.86	$885.09	$925.32
9.5%	$798.82	$840.86	$882.90	$924.94	$966.99
10.0%	$833.70	$877.58	$921.46	$965.33	$1,009.21
10.5%	$869.01	$914.74	$960.48	$1,006.22	$1,051.96

| 11.0% | $904.71 | $952.33 | $999.94 | $1,047.56 | $1,095.18 |

Interest		Principal Amounts Amortized Over 30 Years			
Rates	$120,000.00	$125,000.00	$130,000.00	$135,000.00	$140,000.00
4.0%	$572.90	$596.77	$620.64	$644.52	$668.39
4.5%	$608.03	$633.36	$658.70	$684.03	$709.36
5.0%	$644.19	$671.03	$697.87	$724.71	$751.56
5.5%	$681.35	$709.74	$738.13	$766.52	$794.91
6.0%	$719.47	$749.44	$779.42	$809.40	$839.38
6.5%	$758.49	$790.09	$821.69	$853.30	$884.90
7.0%	$798.37	$831.63	$864.90	$898.16	$931.43
7.5%	$839.06	$874.02	$908.98	$943.94	$978.91
8.0%	$880.52	$917.21	$953.90	$990.59	$1,027.28
8.5%	$922.70	$961.15	$999.59	$1,038.04	$1,076.48
9.0%	$965.55	$1,005.78	$1,046.01	$1,086.25	$1,126.48
9.5%	$1,009.03	$1,051.07	$1,093.12	$1,135.16	$1,177.20
10.0%	$1,053.09	$1,096.97	$1,140.85	$1,184.73	$1,228.61
10.5%	$1,097.69	$1,143.43	$1,189.17	$1,234.90	$1,280.64
11.0%	$1,142.79	$1,190.41	$1,238.03	$1,285.64	$1,333.26

Mortgage/Loan Payment Comparison Table - Payments Made Monthly

Interest		Principal Amounts Amortized Over 30 Years			
Rates	$145,000.00	$150,000.00	$155,000.00	$160,000.00	$165,000.00
4.0%	$692.26	$716.13	$740.00	$763.87	$787.74
4.5%	$734.70	$760.03	$785.37	$810.70	$836.04
5.0%	$778.40	$805.24	$832.08	$858.92	$885.76
5.5%	$823.30	$851.69	$880.08	$908.47	$936.86
6.0%	$869.35	$899.33	$929.31	$959.29	$989.26
6.5%	$916.50	$948.11	$979.71	$1,011.31	$1,042.92
7.0%	$964.69	$997.96	$1,031.22	$1,064.49	$1,097.75
7.5%	$1,013.87	$1,048.83	$1,083.79	$1,118.75	$1,153.71
8.0%	$1,063.96	$1,100.65	$1,137.34	$1,174.03	$1,210.72
8.5%	$1,114.93	$1,153.38	$1,191.82	$1,230.27	$1,268.71
9.0%	$1,166.71	$1,206.94	$1,247.17	$1,287.40	$1,327.63
9.5%	$1,219-24	$1,261.29	$1,303.33	$1,345.37	$1,387.41
10.0%	$1,272.48	$1,316.36	$1,360.24	$1,404.12	$1,448.00
10.5%	$1,326.38	$1,372.11	$1,417.85	$1,463.59	$1,509.32
11.0%	$1,380.87	$1,428.49	$1,476.11	$1,523.72	$1,571.34

Interest Rates	Principal Amounts Amortized Over 30 Years				
	$170,000.00	$175,000.00	$180,000.00	$185,000.00	$190,000.00
4.0%	$811.61	$835.48	$859.35	$883.22	$907.09
4.5%	$861.37	$886.70	$912.04	$937.37	$962.71
5.0%	$912.60	$939.44	$966.28	$993.13	$1,019.97
5.5%	$965.25	$993.64	$1,022.03	$1,050.41	$1,078.80
6.0%	$1,019.24	$1,049.22	$1,079.20	$1,109.17	$1,139.15
6.5%	$1,074.52	$1,106.12	$1,137.73	$1,169.33	$1,200.93
7.0%	$1,131.02	$1,164.28	$1,197.55	$1,230.81	$1,264.08
7.5%	$1,188.67	$1,223.63	$1,258.59	$1,293.55	$1,328.51
8.0%	$1,247.40	$1,284.09	$1,320.78	$1,357.47	$1,394.16
8.5%	$1,307.16	$1,345.60	$1,384.05	$1,422.49	$1,460.94
9.0%	$1,367.86	$1,408.09	$1,448.33	$1,488.56	$1,528.79
9.5%	$1,429.46	$1,471.50	$1,513.54	$1,555.59	$1,597.63
10.0%	$1,491.88	$1,535.76	$1,579.63	$1,623.51	$1,667.39
10.5%	$1,555.06	$1,600.80	$1,646.54	$1,692.27	$1,738.01
11.0%	$1,618.95	$1,666.57	$1,714.19	$1,761.80	$1,809.42

Interest Rates	Principal Amounts Amortized Over 30 Years				
	$195,000.00	$200,000.00	$205,000.00	$210,000.00	$215,000.00
4.0%	$930.96	$954.84	$978.71	$1,002.58	$1,026.45
4.5%	$988.04	$1,013.38	$1,038.71	$1,064.04	$1,089.38
5.0%	$1,046.81	$1,073.65	$1,100.49	$1,127.33	$1,154.17
5.5%	$1,107.19	$1,135.58	$1,163.97	$1,192.36	$1,220.75
6.0%	$1,169.13	$1,199.11	$1,229.08	$1,259.06	$1,289.04
6.5%	$1,232.54	$1,264.14	$1,295.74	$1,327.35	$1,358.95
7.0%	$1,297.34	$1,330.61	$1,363.88	$1,397.14	$1,430.41
7.5%	$1,363.47	$1,398.43	$1,433.39	$1,468.36	$1,503.32
8.0%	$1,430.85	$1,467.53	$1,504.22	$1,540.91	$1,577.60
8.5%	$1,499.39	$1,537.83	$1,576.28	$1,614.72	$1,653.17
9.0%	$1,569.02	$1,609.25	$1,649.48	$1,689.71	$1,729.94
9.5%	$1,639.67	$1,681.71	$1,723.76	$1,765.80	$1,807.84
10.0%	$1,711.27	$1,755.15	$1,799-03	$1,842.91	$1,886.78
10.5%	$1,783.75	$1,829.48	$1,875.22	$1,920.96	$1,966.69
11.0%	$1,857.04	$1,904.65	$1,952.27	$1,999.88	$2,047.50

Mortgage/Loan Payment Comparison Table - Payments Made Monthly

Interest Rates	Principal Amounts Amortized over 30 Years				
	$230,000.00	$235,000.00	$240,000.00	$245,000.00	$250,000.00
4.0%	$1,098.06	$1,121.93	$1,145.80	$1,169.67	$1,193.54
4.5%	$1,165.38	$1,190.72	$1,216.05	$1,241.38	$1,266.72
5.0%	$1,234.69	$1,261.54	$1,288.38	$1,315.22	$1,342.06
5.5%	$1,305.92	$1,334.31	$1,362.70	$1,391.09	$1,419.48
6.0%	$1,378.97	$1,408.95	$1,438.93	$1,468.90	$1,498-88
6.5%	$1,453.76	$1,485.36	1,516.97	$1,548.57	$1,580.18
7.0%	$1,530.20	$1,563.47	$1,596.73	$1,630.00	$1,663.26
7.5%	$1,608.20	$1,643.16	$1,678.12	$1,713.08	$1,748.04
8.0%	$1,687.66	$1,724.35	$1,761.04	$1,797.73	$1,834.42
8.5%	$1,768.51	$1,806.95	$1,845.40	$1,883.84	$1,922.29
9.0%	$1,850.64	$1,890.87	$1,931.10	$1,971.33	$2,011.56
9.5%	$1,933.97	$1,976.01	$2,018.06	$2,060.10	$2,102.14
10.0%	$2,018.42	$2,062.30	$2,106.18	$2,150.06	$2,193.93
10.5%	$2,103.91	$2,149.64	$2,195.38	$2,241-12	$2,286.85
11.0%	$2,190.35	$2,237.96	$2,285.58	$2,333.20	$2,380.81

Interest Rates	Principal Amounts Amortized over 30 Years				
	$255,000.00	$260,000.00	$265,000.00	$270,000.00	$275,000.00
4.0%	$1,217.41	$1,241.28	$1,265.16	$1,289.03	$1,312.90
4.5%	$1,292.05	$1,317.39	$1,342.72	$1,368.06	$1,393.39
5.0%	$1,368.90	$1,395.74	$1,422.58	$1,449.42	$1,476.26
5.5%	$1,447.87	$1,476.26	$1,504.65	$1,533.04	$1,561.42
6.0%	$1,528.86	$1,558.84	$1,588.81	$1,618.79	$1,648.77
6.5%	$1,611.78	$1,643.38	$1,674.99	$1,706.59	$1,738.19
7.0%	$1,696.53	$1,729.79	$1,763.06	$1,796.32	$1,829.59
7.5%	$1,783.00	$1,817.96	$1,852.92	$1,887.88	$1,922.84
8.0%	$1,871.10	$1,907.79	$1,944.48	$1,981.17	$2,017.86
8.5%	$1,960.73	$1,999.18	$2,037.63	$2,076.07	$2,114.52
9.0%	$2,051.79	$2,092.02	$2,132.25	$2,172.49	$2,212.72
9.5%	$2,144.18	$2,186.23	$2,228.27	$2,270.31	$2,312.35
10.0%	$2,237.81	$2,281.69	$2,325.57	$2,369.45	$2,413.33
10.5%	$2,332.59	$2,378.33	$2,424.06	$2,469.80	$2,515.54
11.0%	$2,428.43	$2,476.05	$2,523.66	$2,571.28	$2,618.89

Interest	Principal Amounts Amortized over 30 Years				
Rates	$280,000.00	$285,000.00	$290,000.00	$295,000.00	$300,000.00
4.0%	$1,336.77	$1,360.64	$1,384.51	$1,408.38	$1,432.25
4.5%	$1,418.72	$1,444.06	$1,469.39	$1,494.73	$1,520.06
5.0%	$1,503.11	$1,529.95	$1,556.79	$1,583.63	$1,610.47
5.51	$1,589.81	$1,618.20	1,646.59	$1,674.98	$1,703.37
6.0%	$1,678.75	$1,708.72	1,738.70	$1,768.68	$1,798.66
6.5%	$1,769.80	$1,801.40	1,833.00	$1,864.61	$1,896.21
7.0%	$1,862.85	$1,896.12	$1,929.38	$1,962.65	$1,995.91
7.5%	$1,957.81	1,992.77	$2,027.73	$2,062.69	$2,097.65
8.0%	$2,054.55	$2,091.23	$2,127.92	$2,164.61	$2,201.30
8.5%	$2,152.96	$2,191.41	$2,229.85	$2,268.30	$2,306.75
9.0%	$2,252.95	$2,293.18	$2,333.41	$2,373.64	$2,413.87
9.5%	$2,354.40	$2,396.44	$2,438.48	$2,480.52	$2,522.57
10.0%	$2,457.21	$2,501.08	2,544.96	$2,588.84	$2,632.72
10.5%	$2,561.28	$2,607.01	$2,652.75	$2,698.49	$2,744.22
11.0%	$2,666.51	$2,714.13	$2,761.74	$2,809.36	$2,856.98

Mortgage/Loan Payment Comparison Table - Payments Made Monthly

Interest	Principal Amounts Amortized Over 30 Years				
Rates	$325,000.00	$335,000.00	$345,000.00	$355,000.00	$365,000.00
4.0%	$1,551.60	$1,599.35	$1,647.09	$1,694.83	$1,742.57
4.5%	$1,646.73	$1,697.40	$1,748.07	$1,798.74	$1,849.41
5.0%	$1,744.68	$1,798.36	$1,852.04	$1,905.72	$1,959.40
5.5%	$1,845.32	$1,902.10	$1,958.88	$2,015.66	$2,072.43
6.0%	$1,948.54	$2,008.50	$2,068.45	$2,128.41	$2,188.36
6.5%	$2,054.23	$2,117.43	$2,180.64	$2,243.85	$2,307.05
7.0%	$2,162.24	$2,228.77	$2,295.30	$2,361.83	$2,428.36
7.5%	$2,272.45	$2,342.37	$2,412.30	$2,482.22	$2,552.14
8.0%	$2,384.74	$2,458.12	$2,531.49	$2,604.87	$2,678.25
8.5%	$2,498.97	$2,575.87	$2,652.76	$2,729.65	$2,806.54
9.0%	$2,615.03	$2,695.49	$2,775.95	$2,856.42	$2,936.88
9.5%	$2,732.78	$2,816.87	$2,900.95	$2,985.04	$3,069.12
10.0%	$2,852.11	$2,939.87	$3,027.63	$3,115.38	$3,203.14
10.5%	$2,972.91	$3,064.38	$3,155.86	$3,247.33	$3,338.80
11.0%	$3,095.06	$3,190.29	$3,285.52	$3,380.75	$3,475.99

Interest Rates	Principal Amounts Amortized Over 30 Years				
	$375,000.00	$385,000.00	$395,000.00	$405,000.00	$415,000.00
4.0%	$1,790.31	$1,838.05	$1,885.80	$1,933.54	$1,981.28
4.5%	$1,900.07	$1,950.74	$2,001.41	$2,052.08	$2,102.75
5.0%	$2,013.09	$2,066.77	$2,120.45	$2,174.13	$2,227.81
5.5%	$2,129.21	$2,185.99	$2,242.77	$2,299.55	$2,356.33
6.0%	$2,248.32	$2,308.27	$2,368.23	$2,428.18	$2,488.14
6.5%	$2,370.26	$2,433.47	$2,496.67	$2,559.88	$2,623.09
7.0%	$2,494.89	$2,561.42	$2,627.95	$2,694.48	$2,761.01
7.5%	$2,622.06	$2,691.98	$2,761.90	$2,831.82	$2,901.75
8.0%	$2,751.62	$2,825.00	$2,898.38	$2,971.75	$3,045.13
8.5%	$2,883.43	$2,960.32	$3,037.21	$3,114.10	$3,191.00
9.0%	$3,017.34	$3,097.80	$3,178-26	$3,258.73	$3,339.19
9.5%	$3,153.21	$3,237.29	$3,321.38	$3,405.46	$3,489.55
10.0%	$3,290.90	$3,378.66	$3,466.41	$3,554.17	$3,641.93
10.5%	$3,430.28	$3,521.75	$3,613.23	$3,704.70	$3,796.17
11.0%	$3,571.22	$3,666.45	$3,761.68	$3,856.91	$3,952.15

Interest Rates	Principal Amounts Amortized over 30 Years				
	$425,000.00	$435,000.00	$445,000.00	$455,000.00	$465,000.00
4.0%	$2,029.02	$2,076.76	$2,124.50	$2,172.24	$2,219.99
4.5%	$2,153.42	$2,204.09	$2,254.75	$2,305.42	$2,356.09
5.0%	$2,281.50	$2,335.18	$2,388.86	$2,442.54	$2,496.23
5.5%	$2,413.11	$2,469.89	$2,526-67	$2,583.44	$2,640.22
6.0%	$2,548.09	$2,608.05	$2,668.00	$2,727.96	$2,787.91
6.5%	$2,686.29	$2,749.50	$2,812.71	$2,875.91	$2,939-12
7.0%	$2,827.54	$2,894.07	$2,960.60	$3,027.13	$3,093.66
7.5%	$2,971.67	$3,041.59	$3,111.51	$3,181.43	$3,251.35
8.0%	$3,118.50	$3,191.88	$3,265.26	$3,338.63	$3,412.01
8.5%	$3,267.89	$3,344.78	$3,421.67	$3,498.56	$3,575.45
9.0%	$3,419.65	$3,500.11	$3,580.58	$3,661.04	$3,741.50
9.5%	$3,573.64	$3,657.72	$3,741.81	$3,825.89	$3,909.98
10.0%	$3,729.68	$3,B17,44	$3,905.20	$3,992.96	$4,080.71
10.5%	$3,887.65	$3,979.12	$4,070.59	$4,162.07	$4,253.54
11.0%	$4,047.38	$4,IA2.61	$4,237-84	$4,333.08	$4,428.31

Mortgage/Loan Payment Comparison Table - Payments Made Monthly

Interest Rates	Principal Amounts Amortized Over 15 Years				
	$70,000.00	$75,000.00	$80,000.00	$85,000.00	$90,000.00
4.0%	$517.79	$554.77	$591.76	$628.74	$665.72
4.5%	$535.50	$573.75	$612.00	$650.25	$688.50
5.0%	$553.56	$593.10	$632.64	$672.18	$711.72
5.5%	$571.96	$612.82	$653.67	$694.53	$735.38
6.0%	$590.70	$632.90	$675.09	$717.28	$759.48
6.5%	$609.78	$653.34	$696.89	$740.45	$784.00
7.0%	$629.18	$674.13	$719.07	$764.01	$808.95
7.5%	$648.91	$695.26	$741.61	$787.97	$834.32
8.0%	$668.96	$716.74	$764.53	$812.31	$860.09
8.5%	$689.32	$738.56	$787.80	$837.03	$886.27
9.0%	$709.99	$760.70	$811.42	$862.13	$912.84
9.5%	$730.96	$783.17	$835.38	$887.60	$939-81
10.0%	$752.23	$805.96	$859.69	$913.42	$967.15
10.5%	$773.78	$829.05	$884.32	$939.59	$994.86
11.0%	$795.62	$852.45	$909.28	$966.11	$1,022.94

Interest Rates	Principal Amounts Amortized Over 15 Years				
	$95,000.00	$100,000.00	$105,000.00	$110,000.00	$115,000.00
4.0%	$702.71	$739.69	$776.68	$813.66	$850.65
4.5%	$726.75	$765.00	$803.25	$841.50	$879.75
5.0%	$751.26	$790.80	$830.34	$869.88	$909.42
5.5%	$776.23	$817.09	$857.94	$898.80	$939.65
6.0%	$801.67	$843.86	$886.05	$928.25	$970.44
6.5%	$827.56	$871.11	$914.67	$958.22	$1,001.78
7.0%	$853.89	$898.83	$943.77	$988.72	$1,033.66
7.5%	$880.67	$927.02	$973.37	$1,019.72	$1,066.07
8.0%	$907.87	$955.66	$1,003.44	$1,051.22	$1,099.00
8.5%	$935.51	$984.74	$1,033.98	$1,083.22	$1,132.46
9.0%	$963.56	$1,014.27	$1,064.98	$1,115.70	$1,166.41
9.5%	$992.02	$1,044.23	$1,096.44	$1,148.65	$1,200.86
10.0%	$1,020.88	$1,074.61	$1,128.34	$1,182.07	$1,235.80
10.5%	$1,050.13	$1,105.40	$1,160.67	$1,215.94	$1,271.21
11.0%	$1,079.77	$1,136.60	$1,193.43	$1,250.26	$1,307.09

Interest | Principal Amounts Amortized Over 15 Years

Interest Rates	$120,000.00	$125,000.00	$130,000.00	$135,000.00	$140,000.00
4.0%	$887.63	$924.61	$961.60	$998.58	$1,035.57
4.5%	$918.00	$956.25	$994.50	$1,032.75	$1,071.00
5.0%	$948.96	$988.50	$1,028.04	$1,067.58	$1,107.12
5.5%	$980.51	$1,021.36	$1,062.21	$1,103.07	$1,143.92
6.0%	$1,012.63	$1,054.83	$1,097.02	$1,139.21	$1,181.40
6.5%	$1,045.33	$1,088.89	$1,132.44	$1,176.00	$1,219.56
7.0%	$1,078.60	$1,123.54	$1,168.48	$1,213.42	$1,258.36
7.5%	$1,112.42	$1,158.77	$1,205.12	$1,251.47	$1,297.82
8.0%	$1,146.79	$1,194.57	$1,242.35	$1,290.14	$1,337.92
8.5%	$1,181.69	$1,230.93	$1,280.17	$1,329.40	$1,378.64
9.0%	$1,217.12	$1,267.84	$1,318.55	$1,369.26	$1,419.98
9.5%	$1,253.07	$1,305.29	$1,357.50	$1,409.71	$1,461.92
10.0%	$1,289.53	$1,343.26	$1,396.99	$1,450.72	$1,504.45
10.5%	$1,326.48	$1,381.75	$1,437.02	$1,492.29	$1,547.56
11.0%	$1,363.92	$1,420.75	$1,477.58	$1,534.41	$1,591.24

143

Mortgage/Loan Payment Comparison Table - Payments Made Monthly

Interest | Principal Amounts Amortized Over 15 Years

Interest Rates	$145,000.00	$150,000.00	$155,000.00	$160,000.00	$165,000.00
4.0%	$1,072.55	$1,109.54	$1,146.52	$1,183.51	$1,220.49
4.5%	$1,109.25	$1,147.49	$1,185.74	$1,223.99	$1,262.24
5.0%	$1,146.66	$1,186.20	$1,225.74	$1,265.27	$1,304.81
5.5%	$1,184.78	$1,225.63	$1,266.48	$1,307.34	$1,348.19
6.0%	$1,223.60	$1,265.79	$1,307.98	$1,350.18	$1,392.37
6.5%	$1,263.11	$1,306.67	$1,393.78	$1,437.33	$1,437.33
7.0%	$1,303.31	$1,348.25	$1,393.19	$1,438.13	$1,483.07
7.5%	$1,344.17	$1,390.52	$1,436.87	$1,483.22	$1,529.58
8.0%	$1,385.70	$1,433.48	$1,481.27	$1,529.05	$1,576.83
8.5%	$1,427.88	$1,477.11	$1,526.35	$1,575.59	$1,624.83
9.0%	$1,470.69	$1,521.40	$1,572.12	$1,622.83	$1,673.54
9.5%	$1,514.13	$1,566.34	$1,618.55	$1,670.76	$1,722.98
10.0%	$1,558.18	$1,611.91	$1,665.64	$1,719.37	$1,773.10
10.5%	$1,602.83	$1,658.10	$1,713.37	$1,768.64	$1,823.91
11.0%	$1,648.07	$1,704.90	$1,761.73	$1,818.56	$1,875.39

Interest Rates	Principal Amounts Amortized Over 15 Years				
	$170,000.00	$175,000.00	$180,000.00	$185,000.00	$190,000.00
4.0%	$1,257.47	$1,294.46	$1,331.44	$1,368.43	$1,405.41
4.5%	$1,300.49	$1,338.74	$1,376.99	$1,415.24	$1,453.49
5.0%	$1,344.35	$1,383.89	$1,423.43	$1,462.97	$1,502.51
5.5%	$1,389.05	$1,429.90	$1,470.76	$1,511.61	$1,552.46
6.0%	$1,434.56	$1,476.75	$1,518.95	$1,561.14	$1,603.33
6.5%	$1,480.89	$1,524.44	$1,568.00	$1,611.55	$1,655.11
7.0%	$1,528.01	$1,572.95	$1,617.90	$1,662.84	$1,707.78
7.5%	$1,575.93	$1,622.28	$1,668.63	$1,714.98	$1,761.33
8.0%	$1,624.61	$1,672.40	$1,720.18	$1,767.96	$1,815.74
8.5%	$1,674.06	$1,723.30	$1,772.54	$1,821.77	$1,871.01
9.0%	$1,724.26	$1,774.97	$1,825.68	$1,876.40	$1,927.11
9.5%	$1,775.19	$1,827.40	$1,879.61	$1,931.82	$1,984-03
10.0%	$1,826.83	$1,880.56	$1,934.29	$1,988.02	$2,041.75
10.5%	$1,879.18	$1,934.45	$1,989.72	$2,044.99	$2,100.26
11.0%	$1,932.22	$1,989.05	$2,045.88	$2,102.71	$2,159.54

Interest Rates	Principal Amounts Amortized over 15 Years				
	$195,000.00	$200,000.00	$205,000.00	$210,000.00	$215,000.00
4.0%	$1,442.40	$1,479.38	$1,516.37	$1,553.35	$1,590.33
4.5%	$1,491.74	$1,529.99	$1,568.24	$1,606.49	$1,644.74
5.0%	$1,542.05	$1,581.59	$1,621.13	$1,660.67	$1,700.21
5.5%	$1,593.32	$1,634.17	$1,675.03	$1,715.88	$1,756.73
6.0%	$1,645.53	$1,687.72	$1,729.91	$1,772.10	$1,814.30
6.5%	$1,698.66	$1,742.22	$1,785.78	$1,829.33	$1,872.89
7.0%	$1,752.72	$1,797.66	$1,842.60	$1,887.54	$1,932.49
7.5%	$1,807.68	$1,854.03	$1,900.38	$1,946.73	$1,993.08
8.0%	$1,863.53	$1,911.31	$1,959.09	$2,006.87	$2,054.66
8.5%	$1,920.25	$1,969.48	$2,018.72	$2,067.96	$2,117.20
9.0%	$1,977.82	$2,028.54	$2,079.25	$2,129.96	$2,180.68
9.5%	$2,036.24	$2,088.45	$2,140.67	$2,192.88	$2,245.09
10.0%	$2,095.48	$2,149.22	$2,202.95	$2,256.68	$2,310.41
10.5%	$2,155.53	$2,210.80	$2,266.07	$2,321.34	$2,376.61
11.0%	$2,216.37	$2,273.20	$2,330.03	$2,386.86	$2,443.69

Mortgage/Loan Payment Comparison Table - Payments Made Monthly

Interest Rates	Principal Amounts Amortized Over 15 Years				
	$230,000.00	$235,000.00	$240,000.00	$245,000.00	$250,000.00
4.0%	$1,701.29	$1,738.27	$1,775.26	$1,812.24	$1,849.22
4.5%	$1,759.49	$1,797.74	$1,835.99	$1,874.24	$1,912.49
5.0%	$1,818.83	$1,858.37	$1,897.91	$1,937.45	$1,976.99
5.5%	$1,879.30	$1,920.15	$1,961.01	$2,001.86	$2,042.71
6.0%	$1,940.88	$1,983.07	$2,025.26	$2,067.45	$2,109.65
6.5%	$2,003.55	$2,047.11	$2,090.66	$2,134.22	$2,177.77
7.0%	$2,067.31	$2,112.25	$2,157.19	$2,202.13	$2,247.08
7.5%	$2,132.13	$2,178.48	$2,224.83	$2,271.19	$2,317.54
8.0%	$2,198.00	$2,245.79	$2,293.57	$2,341.35	$2,389.14
8.5%	$2,264.91	$2,314.14	$2,363.38	$2,412.62	$2,461.85
9.0%	$2,332.82	$2,383.53	$2,434.24	$2,484.9	$2,535.67
9.5%	$2,401.72	$2,453.93	$2,506.14	$2,558.36	$2,610.57
10.0%	$2,471.60	$2,525.33	$2,579.06	$2632.79	$2,686.52
10.5%	$2,542.42	$2,597.69	$2,652.96	$2,708.23	$2,763.50
11.0%	$2,614.18	$2,671.01	$2,727.84	$2,784.67	$2,841.50

Interest Rates	Principal Amounts Amortized Over 15 Years				
	$255,000.00	$260,000.00	$265,000.00	$270,000.00	$275,000.00
4.0%	$1,886.21	$1,923.19	$1,960.18	$1,997.16	$2,034.15
4.5%	$1,950.74	$1,988.99	$2,027.24	$2,065.49	$2,103.74
5.0%	$2,016.53	$2,056.07	$2,095.61	$2,135.15	$2,174.69
5.5%	$2,083.57	$2,124.42	$2,165.28	$2,206.13	$2,246.98
6.0%	$2,151.84	$2,194.03	$2,236.23	$2,278.42	$2,320.61
6.5%	$2,221.33	$2,264.88	$2,308.44	$2,351.99	$2,395.55
7.0%	$2,292.02	$2,336.96	$2,381.90	$2,426.84	$2,471.78
7.5%	$2,363.89	$2,410.24	$2,456.59	$2,502.94	$2,549.29
8.0%	$2,436.92	$2,484.70	$2,532.48	$2,580.27	$2,628.05
8.5%	$2,511.09	$2,560.33	$2,609.56	$2,658.80	$2,708.04
9.0%	$2,586.38	$2,637.10	$2,687.81	$2,738.52	$2,789.24
9.5%	$2,662.78	$2,714.99	$2,767.20	$2,819.41	$2,871.62
10.0%	$2,740.25	$2,793.98	$2,847.71	$2,901.44	$2,955.17
10.5%	$2,818.77	$2,874.04	$2,929.31	$2,984.58	$3,039.85
11'.0%	$2,898.33	$2,955.16	$3,011.99	$3,068.82	$3,125.65

Interest Rates	Principal Amounts Amortized Over 15 Years				
	$280,000.00	$285,000.00	$290,000.00	$295,000.00	$300,000.00
4.0%	$2,071.13	$2,108.12	$2,145.10	$2,182.08	$2,219.07
4.5%	$2,141.99	$2,180.24	$2,218.49	$2,256.74	$2,294.98
5.0%	$2,214.23	$2,253.77	$2,293.31	$2,332.85	$2,372.39
5.5%	$2,287.84	$2,328.69	$2,369.55	$2,410.40	$2,451.26
6.0%	$2,362.80	$2,405.00	$2,447.19	$2,489.38	$2,531.58
6.5%	$2,439.11	$2,482.66	$2,526.22	$2,569.77	$2,613.33
7.0%	$2,516.72	$2,561.67	$2,606.61	$2,651.55	$2,696.49
7.5%	$2,595.64	$2,641.99	$2,688.34	$2,734.69	$2,781.04
8.0%	$2,675.83	$2,723.61	$2,771.40	$2,819.18	$2,866.96
8.5%	$2,757.28	$2,806.51	$2,855.75	$2,904.99	$2,954.22
9.0%	$2,839.95	$2,890.66	$2,941.38	$2,992.09	$3,042.80
9.5%	$2,923.83	$2,976.05	$3,028.26	$3,080.47	$3,132.68
10.0%	$3,008.90	$3,062.63	$3,116.36	$3,170.09	$3,223.82
10.5%	$3,095.12	$3,150.39	$3,205.66	$3,260.93	$3,316.20
11.0%	$3,182.48	$3,239.31	$3,296.14	$3,352.97	$3,409.80

Mortgage/Loan Payment Comparison Table - Payments Made Monthly

Interest Rates	Principal Amounts Amortized Over 15 Years				
	$325,000.00	$335,000.00	$345,000.00	$355,000.00	$365,000.00
4.0%	$2,403.99	$2,477.96	$2,551.93	$2,625.90	$2,699.87
4.5%	$2,486.23	$2,562.73	$2,639.23	$2,715.73	$2,792.23
5.0%	$2,570.08	$2,649.16	$2,728.24	$2,807.32	$2,886.40
5.5%	$2,655.53	$2,737.23	$2,818.94	$2,900.65	$2,982.36
6.0%	$2,742.54	$2,826.93	$2,911.31	$2,995.70	$3,080.08
6.5%	$2,831.10	$2,918.21	$3,005.33	$3,092.44	$3,179.55
7.0%	$2,921.20	$3,011.08	$3,100.96	$3,190.85	$3,280.73
7.5%	$3,012.80	$3,105.50	$3,198.20	$3,290.90	$3,383.60
8.0%	$3,105.87	$3,201.44	$3,297.00	$3,392.57	$3,488.14
8.5%	$3,200.41	$3,298.88	$3,397.36	$3,495.83	$3,594.30
9.0%	$3,296.37	$3,397.80	$3,499.22	$3,600.65	$3,702.08
9.5%	$3,393.74	$3,498.16	$3,602.58	$3,707.00	$3,811.43
10.0%	$3,492.47	$3,599.93	$3,707.39	$3,814.85	$3,922.31
10.5%	$3,592.55	$3,703.09	$3,813.63	$3,924.17	$4,034.71
11.0%	$3,693.95	$3,807.60	$3,921.26	$4,034.92	$4,148.58

Interest	Principal Amounts Amortized Over 15 Years				
Rates	$375,000.00	$385,000.00	$395,000.00	$405,000.00	$415,000.00
4.0%	$2,773.83	$2,847.80	$2,921.77	$2,995.74	$3,069.71
4.5%	$2,868.73	$2,945.23	$3,021.73	$3,098.23	$3,174.73
5.0%	$2,965.48	$3,044.56	$3,123.64	$3,202.72	$3,281.80
5.5%	$3,064.07	$3,145.78	$3,227.48	$3,309.19	$3,390.90
6.0%	$3,164.47	$3,248.85	$3,333.24	$3,417.63	$3,502.01
6.5%	$3,266.66	$3,353.77	$3,440.88	$3,527.99	$3,615.10
7.0%	$3,370.61	$3,460.49	$3,550.38	$3,640.26	$3,730.14
7.5%	$3,476.30	$3,569.00	$3,661.70	$3,754.41	$3,847.11
8.0%	$3,583.70	$3,679.27	$3,774.83	$3,870.40	$3,965.96
8.5%	$3,692.78	$3,791.25	$3,889.73	$3,988.20	$4,086.67
9.0%	$3,803.50	$3,904.93	$4,006.36	$4,107.78	$4,209.21
9.5%	$3,915.85	$4,020.27	$4,124.69	$4,229.11	$4,333.54
10.0%	$4,029.77	$4,137.23	$4,244.70	$4,352.16	$4,459.62
10.5%	$4,145.25	$4,255.79	$4,366.33	$4,476.87	$4,587.41
11.0%	$4,262.24	$4,375.90	$4,489.56	$4,603.22	$4,716.88

Interest	Principal Amounts Amortized Over 15 Years				
Rates	$425,000.00	$435,000.00	$445,000.00	$455,000.00	$465,000.00
4.0%	$3,143.68	$3,217.65	$3,291.62	$3,365.59	$3,439.55
4.5%	$3,251.23	$3,327.73	$3,404.23	$3,480.72	$3,557.22
5.0%	$3,360.88	$3,439.96	$3,519.04	$3,598.12	$3,677.20
5.5%	$3,472.61	$3,554.32	$3,636.03	$3,717.73	$3,799.44
6.0%	$3,586.40	$3,670.78	$3,755.17	$3,839.55	$3,923.94
6.5%	$3,702.21	$3,789.32	$3,876.43	$3,963.54	$4,050.65
7.0%	$3,820.03	$3,909.91	$3,999.79	$4,089.67	$4,179.56
7.5%	$3,939.81	$4,032.51	$4,125.21	$4,217.91	$4,310.61
8.0%	$4,061.53	$4,157.09	$4,252.66	$4,348.22	$4,443.79
8.5%	$4,185.15	$4,283.62	$4,382.10	$4,480.57	$4,579.04
9.0%	$4,310.64	$4,412.06	$4,513.49	$4,614.92	$4,716.34
9.5%	$4,437.96	$4,542.38	$4,646.80	$4,751.23	$4,855.65
10.0%	$4,567.08	$4,674.54	$4,782.00	$4,889.46	$4,996.92
10.5%	$4,697.95	$4,808.49	$4,919.03	$5,029.57	$5,140.11
11.0%	$4,830.54	$4,944.20	$5,057.86	$5,171.52	$5,285.18

Appendix B

Schedule of Real Estate Owned

PROPERTY ADDRESS	TYPE & STATUS	DATE & ACQUISTION COST	MARKET VALUE	MORTGAGE HOLDER ADDRESS AND LOAN #	MORTGAGE BALANCE	MONTHLY PAYMENT	MONTHLY TAXES & INSURANCE	GROSS INCOME	NET INCOME
								VACANCY =	
								VACANCY =	

NET INCOME =

SIGNED: _____

SIGNED: _____   DATE: _____

Appendix C

Table of Estimated Closing Costs

ESTIMATED CLOSING COST

Although loan cost will vary - using this matrix will give you a quick
reference to confirm whether the fees you are being quoted are reasonable.

* All figures are based on 7½% interest rate

	50000	100000	125000	150000	175000	200000	225000	250000	275000	300000	325000	350000
Loan Fee %	2%	1.75%	1.5%	1.25%	1.25%	1.25%	1%	1%	1%	1%	1%	1%
Loan Fee $	1000	1750	1875	1875	2187	2500	2250	2500	2750	3000	3250	3500
Proc. Fee	300	300	300	300	300	300	300	300	300	300	300	300
Under Fee	350	350	350	350	350	350	350	350	350	350	350	350
Appra Fee	300	350	350	350	350	350	350	350	350	350	350	350
Credi Fee	50	50	50	50	50	50	50	50	50	50	50	50
Tax Servc	85	85	85	85	85	85	85	85	85	85	85	85
Intrs a day	–	20.83	26.04	31.25	36.45	41.67	46.88	52.08	57.29	62.50	67.71	72.92
Intrs @ %	–\ 333	7.5%\ 625	7.5%\ 781	7.5%\ 937.5	7.5%\ 1094	7.5%\ 1250	7.5%\ 1406	7.5%\ 15625	7.5%\ 1719	7.5%\ 1875	7.5%\ 2031	7.5%\ 2188
Mrtg Ins.	–	–	–	–	–	–	–	–	–	–	–	–
Escrw Fee	350	350	350	350	375	400	425	450	475	500	525	550
Sub-E Fee	125	125	125	125	125	125	125	125	125	125	125	125
Title Ins.	360	450	505	560	612	670	720	775	815	864	910	955
Recon Fee	50	50	50	50	–	–	50	50	50	50	50	50
Recor Fee	50	50	50	50	50	50	50	50	50	50	50	50
Docum Fee	200	200	200	200	200	200	200	200	200	200	200	200
Msngr Fee	–	–	–	–	–	–	–	–	–	–	–	–
Wire Fee	50	50	50	50	50	50	50	50	50	50	50	50
Tax Impou	–	–	–	–	–	–	–	–	–	–	–	–
Insur Impou	–	–	–	–	–	–	–	–	–	–	–	–
Misc.	–	100	100	100	100	100	100	100	100	100	100	100
Misc.	–	100	100	100	225	225	100	100	100	100	100	100
Total Est.	3663	4985	5321	5532	6028	6580	6661	7097	7569	8049	8526	9003
Less Intrs	333	625	781	934	1094	1250	1406	1562	1719	1875	2031	2188
Est. Chrgs	3330	4360	4540	4595	4934	5330	5255	5535	5850	6174	6495	6815

Appendix D
Closing Agents by State

STATE	ATTORNEY	TITLE CO.	ESCROW	COMMENTS
Alabama	x			
Alaska		x		Or mortgage co.
Arizona			x	
Arkansas		x		
California		x	x	Northern: title
Colorado		x		
Connecticut	x			
Delaware	x			
Florida	x	x		Either
Georgia	x			
Hawaii			x	
Idaho		x		
Illinois	x			
Indiana		x		
Iowa	x			

STATE	ATTORNEY	TITLE CO.	ESCROW	COMMENTS
Kansas		X		
Louisiana	X	X		Or mortgage co.
Maine		X		
Maryland		X		
Massachusetts	X			Who hires title
Michigan		X		
Minnesota		X		
Mississippi	X			
Missouri		X		
Montana		X		Or mortgage co.
Nebraska		X	X	Are together
New Hampshire	X			
New Jersey	X	X		Southern: title
New Mexico		X		
New York	X			

STATE	ATTORNEY	TITLE CO.	ESCROW	COMMENTS
North Carolina	x			
Ohio		x		Or mortgage co.
Oklahoma	x			
Oregon			x	
Pennsylvania		x		
Rhode Island		x		
South Carolina	x			
South Dakota		x		Or mortgage co.
Tennessee				Mortgage co.
Texas		x		
Utah		x		
Vermont	x			
Virginia	x	x		Either
Washington	x			
West Virginia	x			
Wisconsin	x			
Wyoming	x			

155

Notes...

Closing Cost Fees Worksheet
(see pages 86-89)

Fees	Cost
Appraisal..	$
Appraisal Review......................................	$
Assignment...	$
Assumption...	$
Credit Report..	$
Demand...	$
Document..	$
Endorsement...	$
Escrow/Settlement....................................	$

158

Fees	Cost
Flood Certification.................................	$
Loan Origination...................................	$
Loan Tie In...	$
Messenger..	$
Mortgage Insurance Premium..................	$
Notary...	$
Pest Inspection.....................................	$
Prepaid Interest..........................	$
Processing..	$

Fees	Cost
Reconveyance...	$
Recording..	$
Sub Escrow...	$
Tax Service Contract..	$
Tax/Insurance Impounds...	$
Title Insurance...	$
Underwriting..	$
Wire Transfer...	$
Misc...	$

160